SI

The Path to Spiritual Excellence

Shaykh Muhammad Nazim Adil
al-Haqqani

Foreword by
Shaykh Muhammad Hisham Kabbani

ISLAMIC SUPREME COUNCIL OF AMERICA

ISBN: 1-930409-18-4

Library of Congress Control Number: 2002109747

Published and Distributed by:

Islamic Supreme Council of America
17195 Silver Parkway, #201 Fenton, MI 48430 USA
Tel: (888) 278-6624
Fax:(810) 815-0518
Email: staff@islamicsupremecouncil.org
Web:http://www.islamicsupremecouncil.org

بِسْمِ اللَّهِ الرَّحْمَٰنِ الرَّحِيمِ

فَلَا أُقْسِمُ بِالشَّفَقِ

وَاللَّيْلِ وَمَا وَسَقَ

وَالْقَمَرِ إِذَا اتَّسَقَ

لَتَرْكَبُنَّ طَبَقًا عَن طَبَقٍ

O, I swear by the afterglow of sunset,
And by the night and all that it enshrouds,
And by the moon when she is at the full,
That ye shall journey on from stage to stage.

Holy Qur'an, Suratu 'l-Inshiqaq, 84: 16-19

Head of the world's largest Naqshbandi Sufi spiritual Order, Shaykh Muhammad Nazim Adil al-Haqqani (right) is the deputy and spiritual heir of Grandshaykh Abd Allah al-Fa'iz ad-Daghestani of Sham (left), whose wisdom and teachings are often referred to in this book. After Grandshaykh Abd Allah's passing from this world in 1973, at his direction Shaykh Nazim began to spread Naqshbandi teachings of the "path to spiritual excellence" to the world-at-large. His lessons dwell on how to discipline the ego, reach a state of spiritual surrender, and achieve true liberation from the bondage of worldly distractions and pursuit.

Shaykh Nazim Adil al-Haqqani (right) is lovingly embraced by his disciple of fifty years, Shaykh Muhammad Hisham Kabbani. In 1990, Shaykh Nazim appointed Shaykh Kabbani to chair several Naqshbandi-Haqqani organizations and to oversee their activities around the world. At the direction of Shaykh Nazim, Shaykh Kabbani has since traveled throughout the Middle East, North America, Europe, Asia, the Pacific Rim, and South Africa, spreading awareness of classical Islamic teachings and principles through publishing, conferences, seminars, community service programs, inter-religious forums, and media relations.

Contents

Foreword

Bismillahi 'r-Rahmani 'r-Rahim

In the name of God, the Compassionate, the Merciful

All praise is due to God the Exalted in bringing yet another luminous volume of Shaykh Nazim's lectures to light. His words and teachings are heavenly wisdom for all, disregarding ethnic and religious barriers to reach the all people. They are special gifts to one who has devoted his heart and life to The Almighty for more than sixty years.

I have been honored to follow Shaykh Nazim since my childhood in Beirut, where he visited my family often. At the tender age of ten years, Shaykh Nazim took me under his wing. He later introduced me to Grandshaykh Abd Allah ad-Daghestani in Sham, who, from our first meeting, became a grandfather figure—always loving and patient.

For more than forty years I have witnessed Shaykh Nazim's furtherance of Grandshaykh Abd Allah's teachings, and the vast audiences from around the world that gravitate to him, always seeking his healing and guidance, his divinely-inspired advice, and his encouragement to serve The Almighty.

The perpetual, far-reaching, and miraculous power of their words and actions continues to impact individual lives and households, and indeed entire communities. Thus, I consider it a distinct privilege to bring their teachings to you, and I pray you receive the benefit of this humble collection of lectures on your personal "path to spiritual excellence."

Shaykh Muhammad Hisham Kabbani
Chairman, Islamic Supreme Council of America
January 1, 2006/Dhu 'l-Hijjah 1, 1426
Fenton, Michigan

About The Author

Since the beginning of human history, God Most High has revealed divine guidance through His prophets and messengers, beginning with the first man, Adam (peace be upon him). The prophetic line includes such well-known figures as Noah, Abraham, Ishmael, Isaac, Jacob, Joseph, Lot, Moses, David, Solomon, and Jesus, ending and culminating in Muhammad, the Seal of the prophets, peace be upon them all, a descendant of Abraham, who brought the final revelation from God to humankind in the sixth century after Christ.

However, although there are no longer prophets upon the earth, the Most Merciful Lord did not leave His servants without inspired teachers and guides. *Awliya*, holy souls or saints, are the inheritors of the prophets. Up to the Last Day these "friends of God," the radiant beacons of truth, righteousness, and the highest spirituality, will continue in the footsteps of the prophets, calling people to their Lord and guiding seekers to His glorious Divine Presence.

One such inspired teacher, a shaykh[1] of the Naqshbandi Sufi Order, is Shaykh Nazim Adil al-Haqqani. A descendant not only of Prophet Muhammad (peace and blessings be upon him) but also of the great Sufi masters Abdul Qadir al-Jilani and Jalaluddin Rumi, Shaykh Nazim was born in Larnaca, Cyprus, in 1922 during the period of British rule of the island.

Gifted from earliest childhood with an extraordinarily spiritual personality, over a period of forty years Shaykh Nazim received his spiritual training in Sham at the hands of Mawlana Shaykh Abd Allah ad-Daghestani (fondly referred to as "Grandshaykh"), the mentor of such well-known figures as Gurjieff and J. G. Bennett. Before leaving this life in 1973, Grandshaykh designated Shaykh Nazim as his successor. In 1974, Shaykh Nazim traveled to London for the first time, thus initiating what was to become an annual visit during the month of Ramadan. A small circle of followers began to grow around him, eagerly taking their training in the ways of Islam and the Sufi Path, *tariqah,* at his hands.

---

[1] A title of honor bestowed on one who has studied within the traditional, centuries-old system of Islamic education, and who is authorized by his mentor to teach others; not to be confused with the perverse application of the term to countless Arab oil tycoons.

From this humble beginning, the circle has grown to include tens of thousands of disciples from all walks of life. Shaykh Nazim possesses a luminous, tremendously imposing spiritual personality, radiating love, compassion, and goodness. He is regarded by many as the *qutb* or "chief saint" of this time.

The shaykh teaches through a subtle interweaving of personal example and talks ("associations," or *suhba*), invariably delivered extempore according to the inspirations that are granted to him. He does not lecture, but rather pours out from his heart into the hearts of his listeners such knowledge and wisdom as may change their innermost beings and bring them toward their Lord as His humble, willing, loving servants.

Shaykh Nazim's language and style are unique; so eloquent, moving, and flavorful, that not only do his teachings seem inspired, but also his extraordinary use of words seems similarly inspired. His association, *suhba,* represent the teachings of a twenty-first century Sufi master, firmly grounded in Islamic orthodoxy, speaking to the hearts of those of any faith who seek God. In a tremendous expression of truth, wisdom, and divine knowledge that is surely unparalleled in the English language, he guides seekers to their Lord's service and exalted pleasure.

The sum total of Shaykh Nazim's message is that of hope, love, mercy, and reassurance. In a troubled and uncertain world in which feeling hearts and thinking minds are constantly disturbed by a sense of things being terribly disordered and out of control, and in which the future seems forebodingly dark and uncertain for humanity, the shaykh proclaims God's love and care for His servants, and invites them to give their hearts to Him.

Shaykh Nazim holds out to seekers the assurance that even their smallest steps toward their Lord will not go unanswered. Rather than threatening sinners with the prospect of Hell and damnation, he offers hope of salvation from the Most Merciful Lord, and heart-warming encouragement and incentive for inner change and growth. As one who has traversed every step of the seeker's path and reached its pinnacle, he offers detailed guidelines for attaining the highest spiritual goals.

In recent years, Shaykh Nazim spends much of his time at his home in Cyprus, surrounded by disciples and visitors from around the world who continue to come and go. Shaykh Muhammad Hisham Kabbani, his disciple of fifty years, now represents Shaykh Nazim and the Naqshbandi-Haqqani Sufi Order throughout the world.

Publisher's Notes

Shaykh Nazim is fluent in Arabic, Turkish, Greek, and semi-fluent in English. Over three decades, his lectures are translated into twenty or more languages, and to date they have reached around the world. We sincerely hope readers will appreciate the author's unique language style, which is painstakingly preserved in this work.

As some of the terms in this book may be foreign, we have provided transliterations throughout, as well as a detailed glossary, a table of the Islamic months and commonly observed holy days.

The term *Allah* is used extensively throughout the book and literally translates to "The One God." Islam teaches that there is only one God for all creation, from before the dawn of time until after its end.

At the conclusion of a lecture, typically Shaykh Nazim says "Fatiha," or "al-Fatiha," which means to recite the first chapter of the Qur'an for its blessing and to seek divine fulfillment of whatever one is asking.

Universally Recognized Symbols

The following Arabic symbols connote sacredness and are universally recognized by Sufi Muslims:

> The symbol ﷾ represents *subhanahu wa ta'ala,* a high form of praise reserved for God alone, which is customarily recited after reading or pronouncing the common name Allah, and any of the ninety-nine Islamic Holy Names of God.
>
> The symbol ﷺ represents *sall-allahu 'alayhi wa sallam* (God's blessings and greetings of peace be upon the Prophet), which is customarily recited after reading or pronouncing the holy name of Prophet Muhammad.
>
> The symbol ﵇ represents *'alayhi 's-salam* (peace be upon him/her), which is customarily recited after reading or pronouncing the sanctified names of prophets, Prophet Muhammad's family members, and the angels.
>
> The symbol ﵁/﵂ represents *radi-allahu 'anh/'anha* (may God be pleased with him/her), which is customarily recited after reading or

pronouncing the holy names of Prophet Muhammad’s Companions.

The symbol ق represents *qaddas-allahu sirrah* (may God sanctify his or her secret), which is customarily recited after reading or pronouncing the name of a saint.

Transliteration

To simplify reading the Arabic names, places and terms are not transliterated in the main text. Transliteration is provided in the section on the spiritual practices to facilitate correct pronunciation and is based on the following system:

Symbol	Transliteration	Symbol	Transliteration	Vowels:	
				Long	
ء	’	ط	ṭ	آ ى	ā
ب	b	ظ	ẓ	و	ū
ت	t	ع	‘	ي	ī
ث	th	غ	gh	Short	
ج	j	ف	f	َ	a
ح	ḥ	ق	q	ُ	u
خ	kh	ك	k	ِ	i
د	d	ل	l		
ذ	dh	م	m		
ر	r	ن	n		
ز	z	ه	h		
س	s	و	w		
ش	sh	ي	y		
ص	ṣ	ة	ah; at		
ض	ḍ	ال	al-/’l-		

Introduction

Bismillahi 'r-Rahmani 'r-Rahim

In the Name of the Lord Almighty, the All-Merciful, the Most Beneficent and Most Magnificent.

This is a good collection of our *suhba* (associations) on various occasions and topics. They are inspirations to a servant of our Lord, the Lord Almighty, coming from our heavenly headquarters, from the spiritual center. I hope they are suitable for curing egos from their illnesses and bad manners, for training and preparing them for the Divine Presence, here and in the Hereafter.

My English is not perfect, but I hope that through the meanings of my words a perfect way of training and teaching is shown. The level of perfection achieved is according to the state of the listeners' hearts, just as the perfection or quality of water depends on its source or origin. Water for drinking may come out of pipes or out of the earth, and spring water is much more attractive for people to run to and drink from than water that runs out of a tap. Therefore, I am trying to take only living words from spiritually authorized people who are in connection with heavens.

In the near future unexpected events are going to take place for which no one can bring an explanation. There are Divine purposes and wisdoms for those events. This is a new beginning. A new period for this world, *dunya*, is coming now.

At that time, for a brief period, all nations are going to carry very heavy burdens. When that finishes, there will be a new opening for all humanity. We are in a tunnel, and until we pass through it, it will get increasingly narrow. Then, when Jesus Christ returns, as is predicted in all Holy Books—the Old Testament, New Testament, and the Holy Qur'an—it will get wider and wider. Only spiritually strong people will pass through this tunnel. Materialist people will not be able to make it; the power of their batteries will be finished.

We have hope, and we are believers; we know that this is only a bridge from one side to another. Only for a short distance, you must pay attention, so that you may pass freely through that valley. Everything depends on belief. Believers should be in safety, worshippers much more, and servants for Allah's Divine Presence should be in full safety.

Events are coming to take away everything that makes humanity artificial. Technology has made people into artificial beings, and their genuine identity has left them. They do not know who they are: animals or angels? Therefore, we are saying people should run back to nature now, to save themselves and to find their true identity.

It is now a big obligation for you to ask to come back to your real personality, to find your identity. It is important now for everyone to try daily for some minutes to be with their own selves, to come to themselves. This is going to be a foundation for a new life for humankind on earth in the third millennium.

Everyone must know what is his or her true value as a human being, and must follow a new way after the destruction of humanities' best qualities. If human beings are not reaching in this very short period the special and valuable qualities that were granted to them by their Creator the Lord Almighty, they are going to sink down. If they quickly run and find them, they are going to be saved.

Shaykh Muhammad Nazim Adil al-Haqqani
8 August 2005
Lefke, Cyprus

1. Association with the Shaykh

Your Private Ocean in the Divine Presence

I seek refuge in God, the Almighty, from Satan's negative influence, and I begin with the Name of God, the Merciful, most Munificent.

I am intending a short association, but I am not in control. My Grandshaykh is over me, and he is spiritually director and controller over me. I may say to you that I am going to make a short association, but it may continue up until morning; it does not matter. Because we are weak people, I am asking forgiveness from our Grandshaykh for me and you; it should be a short address to you.

Association with the shaykh is one of the most important pillars of the most distinguished Naqshbandi Order; it must be. It is like fuel for the car, and believers are in need to move towards the Lord Almighty, towards the heavens. We have been ordered and offered, and we have been called, to move towards the heavens, not to stay on this wild world, not asking to live on this earth for a hundred years and more—no. It is not a genuine target to live longer; but our aim must be to worship as much as possible, more and more. If we are asking for a long life, we are asking only for that purpose: to pray and worship, to obey the Lord of the heavens' commands, and to ask from His endless mercy oceans.

This is a true aim for everyone, a true target for the followers of all religions. If you ask someone, "Would you like to live a long life?" he may say, "Yes." Then we may ask, "Why are you asking for a long life?" "To eat and drink more."

That is the life of animals. It is not an aim to say, "I am asking for a long life for my ego to enjoy this life." Cattle and sheep, what are they asking to live for? To eat as much green grass as possible and that is their only aim. So if you are asking for a long life to enjoy eating and drinking, you have the same aim, and you are going to be on the same level.

But if you are answering, "I am asking for a long life in my Lord's service, for His worship, because it gives me honor. As long as I am alive, my honor is increasing. That is my aim." Which of these positions is excellent? Do you think any religion may refuse what Islam is saying? They cannot. Therefore, excellence is for Islam.

In addition, in Islam it is the most distinguished Naqshbandi Order, which is saying clearly and freely that we are asking for a long life to reach more honor in the Divine Presence through our divine service, serving our Lord. Is anything wrong with this?

Therefore, this is a helpful association that is giving people new refreshment and power to continue with their Lord's divine service. Cars never run without fuel, and believers cannot move without association with the shaykh. Association with a connected person means someone joining with another person to be carried by his power from the earth to the heavens. This is one meaning of association: that you may join the caravan of prophets and saints moving towards their Lord's divine service, Divine Presence. Association is like a hook carrying people from the lowest life to the highest. It is a very important pillar of the most distinguished Naqshbandi Order.

Even if only two or three brothers or sisters, followers of this Sufi Way, *Tariqah,* are together, one of them must say something in their association, and the others must listen.

Our direction, our last destination, is the Divine Presence. Up to there we must move, as rivers run through the land without stopping, until they reach the ocean. So many rivers run in different directions to the ocean. When they reach to the ocean their waters no longer run, there is no more movement, finished. the Lord Almighty is saying:

O My servants, you are moving, you are running, doing this, doing that, until you reach My Divine Presence.[2]

What you are doing is making the waters to approach the ocean. Lakes are not running, but rivers are, and when they reach the ocean, they reach their aim.

Our aim, everyone's aim, is only to reach the oceans in the Divine Presence, and there are endless kinds of oceans. There is not only one ocean, but there may be one for everyone, and he or she must run to reach his or her own ocean; then, they will have arrived at a higher station.

---

[2] C.f. Suratu 'l-Inshiqaq, 84:6.

As a man running after a beautiful lady, when he wins her heart, finished! Women are oceans for men. Men run after them, and when they reach them, they are in their oceans. It is important. Everyone is running to his ocean, and it is only one drop from your ocean that you have been granted in this life, a little bit. That one drop is enough to give you confidence to come to the ocean. What about when you are reaching that drop's ocean in the Divine Presence, that you have been granted? You are swimming in it.

Good tidings! Run to reach your ocean, your last destination in this life. But mindless people now are leaving the ocean. They are going to the desert and, seeing a mirage on the horizon, they run to reach it to find something, but nothing is there, and they are finished. O people, leave the mirage in the desert and come to your ocean; that is for you forever, your last destination in the Divine Presence: love oceans, beauty oceans, endless, tasteful, sweet oceans, that you have been granted from your Lord the Lord Almighty.

Whoever runs after grass and meadows are like cattle, an unexpected and sad fate is awaiting them. But whoever is running after those oceans in the Divine Presence, endless enjoyments are waiting for them, endless tastes, endless blessings, endless favors. You must decide which one is good for you. May God give us a mind to think about it.

What Grandshaykh is giving to us here is not written in books. It is from the pearls of the divine oceans of reality and wisdom; take it and keep it carefully.

Wa min Allah at-Tawfiq. Al-Fatiha.[3]

Ask, and I Shall Give You

(And the angels said,) Praise be to You, we have no knowledge except that which You taught us; You are the Knowing, the Wise One.[4]

---

[3] "Success is with God." Suratu 'l-Fatiha, the first chapter of the Holy Qur'an, is recited in seeking God's blessing and success.

[4] Suratu 'l-Baqara, 2:32.

God is Greatest! O Knowing One, O Wise One, teach us what is beneficial for us and increase our knowledge always!

This is the most distinguished Naqshbandi Order and its main pillar is association[5] with the shaykh. We are asking, and they are giving. If we do not ask, they will not give.

The Lord Almighty is saying, *"Ask and I shall give you."*[6]

First, you must know what you are asking for.

There was once a person who went to a great sultan. When he came to him he brought something as a gift, so that the sultan was very happy with him. He said, "I am pleased with you. Ask, and whatever you ask for, I will grant to you. Immediately I will give it to you."

So that person was thinking, "What may I ask for? My donkey is very hungry, and I have no straw." He asked, "O Sultan, give me a big bag of straw." Such a clever one! Do you understand the foolishness of that person?

The sultan was wondering if that person was crazy, mad, mindless?

"Give him what he is asking for. Give him ten bags of straw, and let him go."

The Lord of the heavens, the Lord Almighty, is watching you when you are asking for something from Him, and most people ask for such nonsense things.

So many people come to me and say, "Tomorrow I am going for an exam, pray for me to pass," or, "I am going to graduate; please pray for my graduation." Every day so many people are coming and saying, "O shaykh, pray for my shop, no one is coming." Another one is asking, "Look for a good job for me, I have no job," or, "O Shaykh, ask for me from the Lord Almighty a little bit more money."

Every day one brother is coming and asking me, "Shaykh, pray for me to have to get married," asking me from the beginning of the day until sleeping time!

---

[5] Arabic: *suhbah.*

[6] Surah Ghafir, 40:60.

So many people come and ask me to pray for this and that—all of it is nonsense. No one is coming and saying, "O shaykh, please pray for me to be an accepted servant in the Divine Presence."

Instead: "Shaykh, please pray for me, because there is an election. I am putting my name down also, let peoples' hearts awake to give their vote to support me, O shaykh."

No one is coming and saying, "O shaykh, pray for me to be closer to the Lord Almighty's most beloved servant, Prophet Muhammad ﷺ, to be his neighbor in Paradise." No one is coming and asking, "O my master, pray for me to be closer to the Lord Almighty."

Therefore, you must ask. However, you must know for what you are asking, and from whom you are asking. If you are going to a village, you may ask for straw there, but it is not right, reaching a sultan's palace, to ask straw from him.

If you are using your mind, it should show you what is true. If you are asking in your heart, your heart may accuse you and say, "I am ashamed in front of the Lord of heavens that you are asking for something that has no value before Him."

O people, you must know about the life on this planet, and you must know about the next life of endless eternity. God the Exalted, likes His servants to ask for eternity. Such a sweet word, "eternity." Even in your language, I like it. *Sermedi,* endless eternity. Ask your Lord, the Lord Almighty, for eternity. Never-ending favors come from Him. Why are you not asking? What are you asking for - something less than straw, much less.

Therefore, sometimes I am ashamed to recite Fatiha only for one person's demand and wish, and I am saying, "O my Lord, I am reciting Fatiha on behalf of him, and for what everyone of Your Beloved Prophet's Nation[7] is asking for with this Fatiha. Grant it to them." I do not like to stop and make one Fatiha for one person only, no. Then it would be like a person asking to hunt, carrying a gun and finding a fly and saying, "I must shoot it!"

"What are you shooting?"

"A fly."

---

[7] Muhammad is the "Beloved" *(habib)* of Allah.

It is a shame to shoot a fly and then try to find it, for it either flew away, or is destroyed and finished.

You are making this temporary life your target, asking to reach something and shooting without reaching that target. You are getting old, before you are granted from the Lord Almighty what you were asking for: towers of Nimrod, one hundred houses, shops, businesses, and companies or an important position. Finally, at the final point of your life, what you were shooting is going to disappear, and you run to look at what you were shooting—looking and finding nothing.

"O, my shooting was so powerful that the target was finished—no sign of it!"

Therefore, it is important for everyone to ask something of value from the Lord Almighty, which He may grant to you. You must make Him pleased, and when He is pleased with you, He will say, "O My servant, everything is for you."

Why you are not trying to make the Lord Almighty pleased with you? Try to make Him pleased, and then He will make you pleased. For every purpose, you should be pleased.

You Must Be Powerful for Faith

May God bless you and give you strong belief, *iman*, and effective actions, so that you are powerful members of the faith. This is important, as the Holy Prophet ﷺ was saying, "A powerful person in religion is better than a weak person."

I seek refuge in God, the Almighty, from Satan's negative influence, and I begin with the Name of God, the Merciful, most Munificent.

We are in need of powerful believers, not weak ones. If we are powerful then Satan should run away, because he fears from powerful people in faith. There are two kinds of powerful people: according to their belief, and according to their physical strength. So many physically powerful people fall down quickly and never give any benefit to the faith. Sometimes you may see a weak person, but he is powerful in his faith, but not in his physical body.

Power comes from the heavens, and heavens grant you as much power from the power oceans as you need. Spirituality is much more powerful than your physical body. The physical being has a temporary existence and you may ask, "How old are you?"

The spiritual being, our soul, no one can speak about it, or ask how old it is—no. No one knows the age of our souls except The Almighty, Who created them.

To be powerful is an order from the saints, and particularly from the Holy Prophet ﷺ. They are asking for powerful believers, and the most powerful believer is the one who can catch the reigns of his ego. Who is not able to keep the reigns of his ego, his ego will throw him away.

Therefore, every association gives a kind of power to the attendee, whether they know it or not. That power is running, but you cannot see it and you cannot hear it. Allah; God, our Lord the Creator, the Greatest One—supreme power oceans are for Him, and eternity is for Him! Everything is coming from God into existence, from pre-eternity up to endless eternity. the Lord Almighty. No part of this life, no piece of material can make His power less.

You must ask for much more power from the Lord Almighty to be strong believers. It is important to be powerful. Do not try to be strong by eating and drinking—cows and oxen are much more powerful than you! If you want to plow, you need ten people on the right hand and ten people on the left to carry the plow through your land.

Another point is to keep the power that you have been granted. A power from the Lord Almighty may reach you and you become powerful, but for some reason you may lose it. This means there is something wrong on your side, something wrong in the sight of the Divine Presence of the Lord. Then even the smallest one of His creatures will make your power less than zero. Keep yourself with power!

It is not easy, because Satan is always attacking you in order to make you weak in front of your ego. Do not listen to him, for then he may carry you to a bad place, with all your power taken in one or two minutes, and you will be left with nothing.

Therefore, sometimes doctors put a patient who is in a very dangerous situation in a room by himself. He may be very ill and weak. If someone comes in without permission, he may catch what that person is carrying.

Therefore, always keep yourself strongly, so that Satan and his orders cannot affect you, and you should be free. May Allah bless you. You are coming to me from one of the furthest places on earth, Argentina. Even Australia is not so far, and Allah rewards you for every step, with so many rewards in Paradise. For your honor, because you have been on pilgrimage, *Hajj*, visiting the House of the Lord, God Almighty rewards you double from born Muslims. Also, because you have been here in this holy month, Muharram, He will reward you with much more, and will open for you the doors of true faith. If you call people to faith, ten, one hundred, or thousands and thousands of people may run after you.

Protect yourself from Satan; be careful of his traps or tricks, so that you do not fall in them. If you feel that you have been caught by Satan, quickly take a shower and pray two cycles[8] of prayer. Ask the Lord Almighty for much more power, so that those dark, narrow, terrible, and nonsense thoughts coming to your heart, should be taken away from you. Then that bad situation will leave you, and you may continue on your way to the Lord Almighty.

If anyone asks you what you are doing, you may say, "We are travelers to the Lord Almighty's Divine Presence."

The Spiritual Power of the Heart

Shah Naqshband[9] said, "The way of our Sufi Path[10] is association with the shaykh, and goodness lies in the group."[11]

This is the root of our Sufi Way, *Tariqah*. The Lord Almighty made Shah Naqshband the main pillar of the most distinguished Naqshbandi Order, and one of the guides that take people on their way to the Divine Presence, so that they are never going to lose their direction towards the Lord Almighty or His teaching. He was saying, "We are teaching people, so that they never lose their way, and their efforts never go without benefit."

It is a short way, a safe way, a happy way. Everyone is walking, moving by themselves. If not time makes them move. So many people are still; only

---

[8] Arabic: *rak'at.*

[9] Shah (the King) Bahauddin Naqshband Muhammad al-Uwaisi al-Bukhari, seventeenth master in the Naqshbandi Golden Chain after Prophet Muhammad ﷺ. The Naqshbandi Sufi Way (*Tariqah*) is named for him.

[10] Arabic: *Tariqah.*

[11] Arabic: *Tariqatuna as-suhba wa 'l-khairu fi' l-jam'iyyah.*

time makes them move. Any moment they may reach to an end, as every beginning must have an end. The movement of people must stop one day, and then they will find themselves in front of two entrances. On one of them is written, "The Way of Paradise," or the way on which people reach to the Divine Presence. On the second entrance is written, "The Way of Hell." Whoever steps through that entrance should be taken to chastisement. There is no safety on that way. It is a very bad end.

Day by day, we are approaching that final destination. One more day has passed. It is going to be one day less, and the day will come when we reach to that entrance. The Naqshbandi Order is taking people in a direction, so that their destination in the end will be Paradise. It is the way of the prophets and the saints, and their inheritors, the Companions of Prophet Muhammad ﷺ, the *Sahaba.* It is difficult for our egos, but happiness for our souls. Everything that is going to be difficult for our egos finally should give us an enjoyment, a pleasure.

Most people are carried on the second way, and Satan is walking ahead of them with his devils and soldiers. Who follows them, finally should reach the entrance to Hell. Why are they going on that way? They are running after it, because their egos are enjoying that way.

If you are not using your willpower, your ego will take you in that dangerous direction. Every association in our Sufi Way, *tariqah,* makes people to pay attention, so they do not follow their ego, but follow the way of the saints and prophets. Every association with the shaykh gives a spiritual power to our soul, so that we may be able to use our willpower against our ego's will. If you are not taking power, spiritual power, it is difficult to prevent yourself from following your ego.

Therefore, we are in need of those people who have spiritual power and who may also give support to our spirituality, so that we can be able to say to our physical demands, to our ego, "No, I am not following you, I am following the way of the saints and prophets!"

Every association gives that power secretly through your soul. Whether you know it or not, feel it or not, does not matter. This power must be given through every association, and it is not important, what we say, or what we hear.

What are we saying here? It means that even if I am reading a newspaper, it does not matter. You are in the operation room, and you are covered. What is important is to attend the association, the presence, of the shaykh, and his spiritual power is going through everyone.

When you are sitting here, blessings are coming from heavens, coming from the Lord Almighty, and those blessings make you powerful. We may say anything through our associations; it does not matter. You heard it or not, you make yourself keep those orders or not. To be here, to attend the association of the Naqshbandi Order, gives you that spiritual power, making your soul to be stronger than your ego. Your spiritual power is increasing, so that you can use your willpower against your ego.

You may think, "I can never remember what the shaykh is saying." The shaykh's address is not to your minds. *'Ulama*, scholars, are addressing your mind; *awliya*, saints, are addressing your souls. Therefore, anytime when you are facing something, what your soul obtained reaches you at that time and gives you that power.

Therefore, association with the shaykh is a most important pillar in the Naqshbandi Order. Always we are under the spiritual supervision of the shaykh, but our physical body also has a right to visit him at least once a year. It may be every week, or every month, or once in forty days, but do not make it longer than forty days between attending an association. This period will keep a person going towards his destination, Paradise.

Now, in our time, there are going to be less and less people, who have been authorized in such a way. If they are not authorized and they are only imitating, it gives power also, but when authorized people make association their full power comes through your hearts, and the heart is the station of The Sultan, Throne of The Sultan. The Sultan's power runs around your physical body to take it towards its direction and destination.

If you are not finding anyone for association, even two disciples can come and sit together. They may say, "I seek refuge in God, the Almighty, from Satan, the rejected, and I begin with the Name of God, the Merciful, most Munificent,"[12] and then one of them can say "There is no god except Allah,"[13] and the other one, "Muhammad is the Prophet of God"[14] asking, "O our Lord, keep us on Your right path, the way of Your prophets, *anbiya*,

---

[12] *A'udhu billahi min-ash shaytan-ir-rajim, Bismillahi 'r-Rahmani 'r-Rahim.*

[13] *La ilaha ill-Allah.*

[14] *Muhammadun rasulullah.*

and saints, *awliya*. Keep us and prevent Satan and devils from affecting us; protect us against their tricks and traps!"

A few minutes are enough, and that mercy may cover them and protect them.

May Allah bless you, shelter our physical bodies, and protect our souls from falling into the hands of devils. May He make a way for those who fall into their hands to save themselves. In addition, we are asking for genuine power for our Naqshbandi Order to collect people, and to move towards the Lord Almighty's Divine Presence. Fatiha.

Ask to Be Closer to the Lord

Shukr, ya Rabbi, Shukr, ya Rabbi, Shukr, Alhamdulillah. Thanks to You O our Lord and all our praise.

Tawbah, ya Rabbi, Tawbah, ya Rabbi, Tawbah, Astaghfirullah. We repent, O our Lord, from all wrongdoing, forgive us.

"The way of our Sufi Path is association with the shaykh, and goodness lies in the group."

This is a new association with shaykh, which makes our friends or our followers improve, and improvement means to become closer to the Divine Presence. This is what we are asking. Only mindless people are asking to be closer to this worldly life, *dunya*, and no one is going to take any benefit from that. But those who are asking to be closer to the Lord Almighty, are reaching what they are asking for from His goodness and blessings.

This is a humble meeting. What we are saying is going to be easily understood. You must ask from the Lord Almighty to be closer to His Divine Presence. No matter how close you get to this worldly life and its treasures, one day you are going to be far away from them—finally you are going to finish. Even if you carry all the keys to those treasures with you, you are not going to look at them. If they bring the most beautiful lady to a man or the most handsome man to a woman, he is not going to look at her; she is not going to look at him.

This means that when you are going to get ready to leave this life and to go back to where you just came from, you are never going to look or to ask for those treasures of this life that you were trying and working so hard to reach. You are going to forget them.

Therefore, every prophet and every saint, particularly Sufi Orders, and among them the most distinguished Naqshbandi Order, are asking to make you run to your Lord and to get closer to Him, even if only by one foot. If you get the chance to come even one foot closer, you must take it. This is the main teaching of the Naqshbandi Order: to encourage people to come closer to the Lord of the heavens.

When the physical body is becoming weaker and you are losing your physical senses, your spiritual being is becoming much more powerful, asking to be closer and to reach to the Divine Presence. But now people are heedless, out of balance. There is a scale: on one side, you have a pearl or diamond, and on the other dung, dirt from animals. People leave the diamond and run to take the dirt. That is heedlessness. Why are you trying to reach so much from this worldly life, and you are not asking to be closer to the Divine Presence and to take much more from there? They have no balance; people have just lost their balance.

Anyone who prefers his temporary life, leaving permanent blessings, is a mindless person. Therefore, the Lord Almighty says that these people are like animals. Not only like animals, but below animals. What is your judgment on a person who chooses this temporary life and its pleasures instead of permanent life and its enjoyments? It means that he has no mind. He is like an animal. the Lord Almighty even says:

Their level is under the level of animals.[15]

We do not know which day is going to be our last day, and it is enough for a person to know that for everyone there is going to be a last day in this life, *dunya.* On that day, you are going to leave everything you collected from the beginning up until that day, and you are getting out, like loading a huge truck, putting everything on it, and driving to the border. There is a stop sign, *qaf*[16], and the guards come and say, "From here onwards only you may pass."

He may ask, "What about my truck?"

But the guards reply, "There is no possibility for your truck to move forward. You must get out down and walk through. Leave everything behind and only you come."

---

[15] Suratu 'l-'Araf, 7:179.

[16] A letter of the Arabic alphabet that in recitation connotes a full stop.

How did you come to this world? You came naked from your mother's womb, and quickly they covered your naked body with something from this life, wrapping you up in clothes. When you are leaving, the guards of the border between this world and the afterlife, *akhira,* will instruct you, "Leave everything there and only you pass through this border."

And you are coming with your white clothes only. You must leave everything else, and you will look, "O, how can I bring this truck? What have I done? My whole life I was running, I did not rest or sleep, I gathered so many things, and now they say that I cannot take any of it. How can I come without them?"

But the guards will say, "Come, come, it is finished. These things are for the people in that area. You cannot bring them to this area."

The Last Day is already appointed. Everyone has an appointment with the postman, the Angel of Death, who takes your soul to its Lord. He is looking in his diary, to see with whom he has an appointment. When your name is appearing, your appointment with him should be on that day, in such and such a place, at such and such a time. And he is coming quickly, carrying a big, big book, in which is written the appointments for all humankind.

He is looking and saying, "Now I am coming to you, it is our appointment."

"How? I do not know about this appointment, I thought there was more time."

"No, it is written here. I am not coming one hour before or one hour after. I am so punctual, I come on time. It is finished, I am taking you now."

"What about my life, my truck, and so many things, what I shall do?"

"Leave that and you come alone."

Those who are closer to the Lord Almighty will be dressed in heavenly dressings, to be taken to the Divine Presence of the Lord, the Lord Almighty. But those who did not prepare themselves for that heavenly dress should be taken away—they cannot be taken to their Lord's Divine Presence. Everyone is waiting for their last day, looking for their last moment, their journey from this temporary life to a permanent life. O people, take much more care for your eternal life. Try to be welcomed in a good way at the last moment when you are leaving this life.

May God bless you and forgive us. Fatiha.

2. Traveling towards Eternity

Coming from God and Going to God

Thanks and praise of God opens the gates of Heaven; repentance and seeking refuge closes the gates of Hell.

Shukr, ya Rabbi, shukr, ya Rabbi, shukr, alhamdulillah. Thanks to You O our Lord and all our praise.

Tawbah, ya Rabbi, tawbah, ya Rabbi, tawbah, astaghfirullah. We repent, O our Lord, from all wrongdoing, forgive us.

"The way of our Sufi Path is association with the shaykh, and goodness lies in the group."

These are the words of Shah Naqshband, may Allah give him much more honor. He was, and still is, guiding the Community of Prophet Muhammadi[17] ﷺ to the Lord Almighty. We are coming from the heavens, from Allah, we are touching this planet, and then we are returning to Him. Nothing else.

When we touch this planet on our way, it is going to be perhaps for one hundred years, or eighty, forty, or maybe just eight years. The period of our lives is going to be different. Countless events are happening in this worldly life, *dunya*, and so many things we are interested in to which we give all our power—and they are all falsehood, *batil.* The Lord Almighty is saying in His Holy Qur'an:

> *We are coming from God and to Him we are returning.*[18]

That is the genuine truth.

---

[17] According to the Naqshbandi Sufi teachings, the Community of Prophet Muhammad ﷺ, who was sent by God as "a mercy to all creation" (*rahmatan li 'l-'alameen*), includes all humankind, not only Muslims.

[18] Suratu 'l-Baqara, 2:156, Arabic: *Inna lillahi wa inna ilayhi raji'oon.* This verse is traditionally pronounced upon hearing of the passing away of someone from this life.

The people of this century never take any interest to find out from where they are coming, and to where they are going. Their only interest is this life, what they are touching in this life up to the time they leave. They think that sixty or seventy years is a lot. And they think that they may enjoy themselves throughout this short lifetime, sixty, seventy years, more or less, for ninety and one-hundred year-old people are so difficult to find.

Where were you before you came to this life? You were in the Lord Almighty's Divine Presence. You are coming from Him; coming a long way. You have forgotten it. What makes you to forget? You are not believing, for if you were, you would have to take an interest in yourself and ask, "What *has* happened, and what is *going* to happen?" But people seldom use their minds to contemplate this; their interest is only in that short time in which they are living.

Everything in this life is directed in such a way that a person is never going to take an interest in his spiritual being and his spiritual life. Everything that has happened, what is happening now, and what is going to happen is only making you not take any interest in your original source, not to ask from where you are coming. This is big trouble for humankind.

You see running water, and you ask, "From where is this river coming? Is it pure or not?" For water, you ask. But for yourself, although you are running day-after-day like rivers, you are not interested to ask, "Where did I come from? Where am I going?" The answer is just as we said: coming from God and going to God.

Our time is very short and full of interests that never leave you to look after anything from your eternal life, and eternal life is to be with the Lord Almighty. He is the Eternal One, and if His servant is asking for eternity, then He dresses him with such lights, with such powers, that step-by-step his interests are going to change. Then finally, he or she reaches a point that they understand where they are coming from and to where they are going. There are plans. On one, it is written "From the Lord Almighty" and on another "To the Lord Almighty."

You must try to be for your Lord. You must try to force your ego to live for God and to learn that you are coming from God and going to Him. Tell your ego, "My interest in you is not for this life, for my interest is only in my Lord. I came and stepped on this planet, and after a while my feet are taken from this earth and directed towards other, perhaps unknown, direction; perhaps where there are no more directions."

O people, he who is going opposite to God's calling is going in the wrong direction. That is why a difficult consequence comes on a person, who understands this, but does not keep it. You must understand, in this short life, everything that has happened, what is happening and what will happen, forever. Be careful what you do here, what you plant here, so that you should be powerful, and full of enjoyment and satisfaction.

O people, try to make your ego say that we are coming from the Lord Almighty, and we are changing crew, taking new fuel, and then leaving towards the heavens in our space ships. Everyone has a vessel, like the Ark that was granted to the Prophet Noah ﷺ. You may enter it and go freely to your Lord's Divine Presence.

May God forgive us and make us understand. It is so clear—to come from God and to go to God. O people, live for Allah, do for Allah, go to Allah, and be for Allah. Fatiha.

Our Final Destination Is the Divine Presence

In the name of God, the Beneficent, most Munificent and Merciful. This is a new association with our Grandshaykh, even though the hour is late. Sleep is sultan, nobody can resist it; but it is also a blessing, *rahmah*.

What shall we do? We must try to translate something to you. It is as necessary for you as food. You are in need of food for your physical body. You must cook and eat what the Lord Almighty created for your physical being, but for your soul, you are in need of spirituality, spiritual food.

This bottle here, if it is full, you may give something from it, but when it is empty what can you give? The ego is only interested in reaching its own targets. People living now are only running after their physical body's interests. Perhaps you may find one out of 10,000, or 50,000, or 100,000 people, who may have an interest in spirituality. And the highest spirituality, which is never decreasing, you can only find through Islam. What the Lord Almighty granted to Prophet Moses ﷺ and to Jesus Christ ﷺ, was something to be given in a limited place and time to their followers. Christianity, from the beginning, tried to give people what they needed for their spiritual life. And therefore Jesus Christ ﷺ was saying, "I am your Lord's servant, nothing else, and that is my honor." Islam came to restore the law of Moses ﷺ and the spirituality of Jesus ﷺ.

Can an ant understand who Man is? Never, not even if it lived for one million years. And as much as men and women may ask for more wisdom and more from the Lord's divine knowledge, what they can take from it is always going to be small. This is because limited things, even though they may appear big in our eyes, are always going to be nothing in the divine oceans of greatness. But people are so crazy, so mad, and so foolish, they are asking to know who God is, or how God is, or where God is. *Ya Hu!*[19]

Where is Italy? Where is Germany? Where is America? Where is Malaysia? Show me! And you are saying, "I cannot show you from here now, but come with me on a plane, and we shall fly and I shall show you my homeland." O donkey, if you are only asking about Malaysia and you are in need to take a plane and fly fifteen hours to land there, and then still you do not know it how you can say, "Show me God."

I am saying, "Show me beyond these skies; show me the beginning of space, its limits, where it ends, then I will show you beyond that." You need thirteen, fourteen or fifteen hours to travel to Malaysia. How many years, or centuries, or billions of years must you fly to find the last point of space? Then I will show you where the Lord is, where His state is. First reach the end of the World of Forms, *'Alam an-Nasut*; the World of Spirits, *'Alam al-Jabarut*; the World of Angels, *'Alam al-Malakut;* the Divine Presence, *'Alam al-Lahut*. But people in their ignorance are asking, "Where is Allah?" He created the where; how can you ask where? He created time; how can you ask His age?

How old is our galaxy? So many billions of galaxies are running. I am saying, ride on one of them; they are all running to their Lord's Divine Presence. Take any one of them, all of them are running in the same direction. Not one galaxy is going in the opposite direction. There are no accidents in heavenly traffic! Take one, and then you may reach with it to the Divine Presence. What is your payment? You must pay, as a ticket, for riding on any galaxy with your physical body. You must give it as a payment. You can ride any galaxy if you are paying. Give your physical body to them, and then every galaxy may take you for free, saluting you, taking you to the Divine Presence.

---

[19] An exclamation in Turkish language.

Where is the Divine Presence? Only Allah, the Owner of the galaxies, may say, "This is the last station for this galaxy. Now it has arrived. I am here!"

Good news for those who can pay for the ticket. Any galaxy may accept you and you may continue on it. Then the Lord of heavens says, "Stop, this is your last destination. I am here. Come to Me." God is most great! He is taking away the the Veil of Greatness, *Hijab ul-'Adhamah.* Supreme Greatness is for the Lord Almighty. These veils open and He says, "I am here." Everywhere, God, the most High, the most Great. Allah, the Knowing, the most Powerful. Everything is in its perfection for Him, the Almighty.

You must understand, it is from eternity to eternity. When the angels ask, "Where are you asking to reach?" you must answer, "I am moving towards eternity."

"Then come, because who is asking for eternity may come."

Who is asking for anything else, the ticket collector will kick him off, "Go! This is only for those who are asking for eternity, go away."

Seek Perfection from a Perfect One

Now we are in this temporary life. Tomorrow, next week, next month, next year, or next century, we are going to leave. We must leave this life and move from this world to another world, which is only described to us by the prophets. No one may open the veils from the coming days, and no one can know what will happen after tomorrow in the endless future. Only He Who created you, humankind, may know what is going to happen in the future, and He is the Only One who can remove the veils.

He is the Creator of the coming days and the Designer of every day's program. Do not think that any day may come by itself without a program, no. Every day must come by His Will, and everything, which is coming into existence, which will appear tomorrow, is programmed by Him with all the details, not only with the headlines.

Yourself and every creature, everything, is representing our Creator's endless power, His endless perfection. It begins with the smallest representative of creatures, which is less than an atom, then continues to the atomic world, the solid world, the plant world, the animal world, the human world, mountains, oceans, the earth, stars, galaxies. Everything shows the Lord's perfection, and He puts perfection in everything, never leaving any imperfection in any creature in any of these worlds.

There is a perfect connection between everything, from the smallest unit in the atomic world, to the gigantic star systems in the world of the galaxies. Nothing and no one can be by itself, by himself or by herself. By that connection, everything in existence knows its Creator. This is a common connection between everything in existence, that they know, or must know, their Creator—heavenly beings, earthly beings, the smallest creatures up to huge, gigantic galaxies. None among the countless creatures is going to deny the existence of their Creator; only completely foolish, intoxicated people will deny it.

The second common connection among everything in existence is that all creatures give their most high and endless respect to their Lord, which is their glorification. Everything must glorify! They are saying that some things are not alive, but everything in existence has a life, and everything is alive with that glorification. If something is not glorifying the Lord, it is going to vanish, finish, it will lose its life. Everything that is coming in existence must glorify its Lord, Allah Almighty. Oceans are glorifying; mountains, earths, skies, sun, moon, stars, galaxies, animals, and plants are glorifying; your body is glorifying. But people, because they are heedless, are not using their tongues to say, *Subhanallah*, "Glory to the Lord Almighty!"

Therefore, the events which are going to happen tomorrow are in their most perfect position. You cannot find any imperfection in anything in existence. Events are in their full perfection, because He who created that event and that creature is in His endless perfection.

Perfection may be taken from a perfect person. An imperfect person cannot give perfection to someone else, because if he is imperfect, he must give from his imperfection. I can only give from what I have. If I have not, what am I going to give you? If I have perfection, I am giving perfection. If I have imperfection, I am giving imperfection.

There is no imperfection with the Lord of the heavens, and He gives to every thing its perfection. He is asking His servants to ask for what they are in need of from Him: perfection. But people ask for this or that. No, ask from Him, from His perfection oceans, to give you perfection, so that you do not come to His Divine Presence in an imperfect condition.

The Lord of heavens may ask, "Why you are coming in such a condition? Why are you not coming to My Divine Presence with perfection? Why are you coming imperfect?"

If the servant says, "I never asked for more than this, I did not know where perfection was," then the Lord Almighty may say:

> O My servant, why did not you look for a perfect one among My servants? If you had asked, you would have found someone, but you never asked, so you never found anyone and you are coming to Me imperfect. If you were asking for perfection from Me, I would have granted it to you, but you did not ask. You asked for this and that, although perfection was the best thing for you to ask for, and the highest honor was to come to My Divine Presence with perfection.

It is so important to ask, and then you can find those people who have perfection. It is not for common people, but if you ask, you can find a perfect servant and he may give to you. But if you are not asking, you will not find one.

This is the meaning of the Prophet's ﷺ saying:

If knowledge is to be found in China, you must run after it.[20]

At that time China was the last known place on earth, beyond which no country was heard of. The Prophet ﷺ knew better, but he was addressing the people in front of him who knew only China as the furthest state. He meant to say, "If you are asking for knowledge, and the person who may teach you that knowledge is in China, run to him."

What kind of knowledge? A knowledge that gives you perfection. Not a kind of knowledge which is only written down to make books, no. There are millions of books. But try yourself; can you take perfection from them? You can? O, very good; but you cannot find the perfection which belongs to you.

There may be a big warehouse full of keys, thousands of keys, and you are in need of a single key, and you are coming and saying, "O keeper of this warehouse of keys, I have lost my door key, give me the key." But he

---

[20] al-Bayhaqi in *Shu'ab al-iman* and *al-Madkhal*, Ibn 'Abd al-Barr in *Jami' Bayan al-'ilm*, and al-Khatib his *al-Rihla fi talab al-hadith*.

does not ask what kind of key it was and what it looked like, he only says, "This is the key," and gives it to you. And you go and try the key, but you cannot open the door. You come back and ask, "Give me another key." But up to the end of the world the keys are never ending and they never open that door.

So there are millions of books full of knowledge, but which one is giving you perfection? You need maybe a million years of lifetimes to try and find out which one is for you. O heedless people, it is never ending. Even in one million years you will not finish. But that person, who is an expert, is saying to you, "What are you asking for? What kind of lock do you have, tell me." Then he is looking and saying, "Bring this key to him."

Therefore, that person must know the perfection that you need. That knowledge may be found in China, but not in books. Genuine knowledge through our hearts is what we are asking for. So that is the wisdom of what the Prophet ﷺ was saying. Knowledge is knowledge, here or in China. But if that person who may give you that perfection is living there, run to him and take from him. He may give you the key to open your treasures.

May Allah forgive us and make us understand something from perfection. Look for His representatives on earth to reach Him. If you do not find them, you cannot reach Him.

Knowledge of the Heart Is Never Lost

The first night of the New Year just began at sunset. We are asking the Lord Almighty to make this year good for faith and for believers everywhere, because believers are now in a very dangerous situation. Unexpected events have happened, events that no one could have imagined.

The world is changing day by day, because it is running at full speed towards its destination, and for every creature there must be a destination. The Lord Almighty does not create anything without its destination, even the smallest one walking or flying.

I am asking scientists and authorized people, experts, about a certain creature on earth. "What is its name? It must have a name." But our foolish and proud scholars do not know and they reply, "It is not written in our books." Scholars are claiming that they know about everything! If I ask, "What is that creature's name?" they reply, "We did not take a photograph of that creature or put it under a microscope. We did not ask its name yet, because we are meeting it for the first time now."

I am saying, "Ask that creature if it knows about you. Ask it, 'Do you know who I am?' And it may say, 'Yes, you are from the Children of Adam!'"

Every creature must know the deputy of the Lord Almighty on earth; this is important. You have never heard such things before. Every creature must know the Divine Deputy, *Khalifatullah*.[21] They have been ordered to know him, also to be obedient, and to be of benefit to him, because nothing is created without giving a benefit to humankind. Everything is created for humankind, and everything is helping humankind by its creation.

Before the creation of humankind, before the coming of the deputy of the Lord Almighty, the creatures were looking and waiting for him, to be obedient to humankind and to help his descendants and give their best to them. Animals, plants, everything on earth, in the earth, in the atmosphere, in the skies, in space, everything is created for humankind! Indeed God is most great!

That small creature also knows about you, because you have been created to be sultan (ruler) over them. And yet you are heedless of your genuine being, not making any research about yourself and the importance of your existence. No, you only make enquiries and research into a few creatures, but you cannot enter the ocean of the Lord's countless beings. They are living everywhere, whether you can see them or not. Everywhere is full of creatures, and they are looking at you, but you cannot see them. They know about you, and you do not have full knowledge about yourself!

An ignorant person may ask, "Does anyone know the names of the creatures?"

The creatures reply, "Yes, the Lord Almighty created Adam to be His deputy, *khalifa* on earth, saying,

He taught Adam the names of every creature that He created.[22]

Prophet Adam ﷺ knew their names fully. For example, here in this room there are maybe one hundred people, and everyone has a name. Your

---

[21] The Lord Almighty appointed Man as His deputy on earth; *khalifatullah*.

[22] Suratu 'l-Baqara 2:31.

common species is human, but individually you are 'Ahmad' (the praised one). Therefore, Adam knew the common names, and also, one-by-one, every creature's individual name.

That is a level for all humanity, and there are specific levels for everyone. When someone is reaching there spiritually, there is an opening. What you put in your mind, even after a long time you may forget. Mind products quickly may be lost, forgotten. However, what you have been granted by the Lord Almighty through His most Respected Servant and Prophet Muhammad ﷺ, what is coming to your soul, you never forget. Mind products are going to melt and finish, but not heart products; they are kept, and they belong to our souls. It is like a fish that is brought to you, and you take this fish and throw it back into the ocean so that it may live there forever. But out of the ocean with you, it cannot live.

Like that, mind products may only be kept for a short time. You may learn something, know it, but then forget it again. But what you have been granted from the Lord Almighty is never going to be forgotten.

It is a very dangerous situation for humankind. People claim to be learned and to know so many things. However, they have also been given forgetfulness, which makes them to lose all of it. All people may forget. No one can say, "I am not forgetting anything," except the *awliya*, the saints, who are keeping knowledge through their hearts, not through their minds.

Who is keeping knowledge in his mind, day by day, little by little, is going to lose it. The problem with knowledge is that anytime it can be forgotten—you are learning, but forgetfulness never lets that knowledge stay with you. However, who keeps knowledge through his heart never forgets! I was with Grandshaykh for forty years, and I never heard him say about anything, "I forgot." Rather he said, "When I was born my heart was working, and knowledge was in it."

O people, you must try, in this time particularly, to save yourself and your family from terrible and horrible events. Take care for them, and it will give you contentment. Do not run after money, for it can never give you any insurance.

Therefore, we are trying to say those holy words *la ilaha ill-Allah, la ilaha ill-Allah, la ilaha ill-Allah*, asking to put it into our heart by repeating it, because through the mind a person may lose it. So many ignorant people are objecting to Sufi people who say and repeat *la ilaha ill-Allah*. They are getting very angry because their teacher is Satan. Every Sufi Way, *Tariqah*, is asking to take that holy word from our minds to our hearts. Hearts never forget, so it is never going to be lost. If you are not keeping calling on God and remembering Him, *dhikr*, you are going to forget after hours or days.

Therefore, Sufi ways are helping people transport their knowledge from their minds to their hearts. It is a little difficult, but you must try to take away the difficulties. The only way to opening hearts is to say *la ilaha ill-Allah.*

Those square-head people never understand and they are resisting, asking, "Why are you making *dhikr*?"

We are making *dhikr,* so the realities that belong to the Lord of the heavens come from our minds to our hearts. Then they are never going to be forgotten, and we may always know them. That is the important point for the Sufi Path.

We have a saying that if you put chocolate in front of a donkey it will refuse it, but if you put straw, it will eat it. What shall we do if people insist on being like donkeys, only happy with straw?

We hope that throughout this year every day a new power will help our sincere leaders rise up, and make the leaders of the enemies of Truth, enemies of heavenly beings, fall down. Ask from Allah day by day to guide you. *Ya Allah* (O God!), grant us the Sultan of Divine Law from Your Divine Presence on earth. Fatiha.

Humankind Has Been Honored with a Divine Trust

The method of our Sufi Way is association with the shaykh, and we are in need of guidance. The first guide of the Community was the most praised, respected and glorified servant of the Lord Almighty, Prophet Muhammad ﷺ. I am asking from my Grandshaykh to grant us a good understanding of who the Holy Prophet ﷺ is.

There is a saying of Arabs before Islam, "Who never keeps something valuable with himself, is going to be an enemy of the one who does." That is a kind of foolishness, because we are not all created the same. The meaning, or method, for the creation of humankind is different from other creatures, as humankind is the Creator's most perfect creature. Those who were not granted that honor became his enemies.

In the beginning, the Lord Almighty gave the good tidings of the creation of His Deputy to the angels. They were innocent and said, "If You like to make a new creature, we accept. If You are making that creature to be on the same level with us, we accept. If You make his honor more than our honor, we also accept."

Satan wanted that honor for himself. When Adam ﷺ had that quality, he and his children became the number one enemy of Satan, who said, "I am not accepting that one. If the rank and position of this new creature is going to be above mine, I am going to be disobedient."

Obedience was an order from the Lord Almighty. Satan had given his oath, his promise to the Lord Almighty, as everyone promised on the Day of Promises, "We will be Your servants."

But Satan did not accept any prophet, trying to keep every honor for himself. He said, "If I am not granted to be above that new creature, I am not going to accept him, I will have no respect for him, and I will never leave him to live happily or to stand up. If he is going to be above me in his rank, I will go against the command of the Lord of heavens. That honor was for me, but it was taken from me and given to that new creature."

Satan was so angry. Therefore, when he was not granted that honor from the Lord Almighty, he became an enemy to Adam and his children. That same characteristic from people to each other is taking them away. That worst characteristic of our egos is to be jealous or envious, and the main source of that is Satan. Whoever is jealous or envious has a part of Satan, and he is not pure. Even though he was given everything, Satan is never happy with humankind. So, he is moving among ignorant groups of people, making them to attack and give trouble to people everywhere. He is laughing. We are in a time of darkness, ignorance, bad characteristics, and faults, a time of cruelty and injustice. All these things also happened before the coming of Islam.

Satan is the number one troublemaker, and first class at harming people. Human beings would be in peace, if there were no Satan. He is making people to go against the commands of the Lord. Every time his teaching to humankind is, "Do not be obedient, live your life, you are coming to this life only once, there is no life after death." He is making people to refuse anything from spirituality, like the fundamentalist, Wahhabi people. Their mind is only for materialism. They try to make a lot of gold and silver, to be the richest, but to be the richest never gives any benefit.

Then they become seventy, eighty years old, and everything is finished. Satan is cheating and knocking people down.

Therefore, if you have some good characteristics and good actions, some animals will object and say, "Why has he been granted that honor and he has only two legs, while we have four legs? How can it be? And we do not know how they are walking with two legs." They did not expect that a person could walk like that. Therefore, Satan was very surprised and sorry to see people run with two legs. So he made a declaration, "Perfection for human beings is to have four legs. Two legs are imperfect." He said, "I will try to take them under my command and make them four legged, but they must not realize this. If they see themselves with four legs, they will leave me and escape, and I must keep them. They have two legs, and I am giving them two more legs to make it four. But still they should doubt if those new things that they are wearing are going to be for them forever, or if those two-leg people riding on horses should come to take away their freedom!"

Therefore, when people lose their values they become enemies of those who have values. Humankind's creation is special, so if people look to each other with a superficial look, they will never be successful in their life. They must understand the genuine value, which they have been granted from the Lord Almighty. Satan lost it and became an enemy to the Children of Adam, who have that honor, and he is always trying to take away that divine trust from our hearts and leave us like animals. That is the trouble going on now in our days, because Satan is saying one thing, but keeping something else in his heart, asking to be 'Number One' over all creatures. He became a first class enemy for every prophet, especially for the Seal of prophets, Prophet Muhammad ﷺ.

Humankind now, step-by-step, little by little, is asking to come to the level of animals, because they think that on that level they should have absolute freedom in their life. This is the first idea or idol of the new generation: to make absolute freedom for themselves and their descendants. Therefore, in the coming days unexpected events should come to humankind, and he should wonder and ask, "What is happening, what is going on?"

In this time thousands of people may be going to die at unexpected times. This means that the young generation should be in danger, because they never take any care for, and never worry about, worshipping the Lord

Almighty. Who is not taking care of the Lord's holy commands may suddenly pass from this life. Death is the heaviest penalty for humankind.

There will be wars, fighting and troubles throughout the coming years; wars, which will not give any honor to people, and which are only for destroying everything, and to harm as much as possible.

May Allah forgive us and bless you. We are asking Divine Support to bring down the satanic kingdom soon. Fatiha.

Depend on God

A man always likes to depend on someone. The most powerful people that you know are rich people, and they think their wealth supports them. But sometimes you see multi-millionaires, whose huge wealth does not give them any enjoyment, because old age came to them and that wealth cannot give them any defense.

Therefore, you must not ask for some kind of power that you are using, and that you invented, no. It is so difficult for technology to defend you. And also, a person who is asking for peace and satisfaction in his life must look for some land, some place, that is going to belong to him only, and does not have any partners.

We seek spiritual support, from Sultanu 'l-awliya, and spiritual support from the close friends of God, *rijalullah*. We are asking forgiveness from the Lord Almighty and we are also giving endless thanks to Him. As much as we are giving more thanks, *shukr*, more honor and lights, *nur*, are coming to us. If a person is not giving thanks, even if he goes to pray the morning prayer in congregation and sits up until the noon prayer, or until the evening and night prayers, it will not be easy for that person to keep his ego and try to fulfill his oath that he gave his Lord on the Day of Promises. All of us gave our oath to God, saying, "We are promising to You that we shall be Your servants for Your heavenly, divine service."

Now everyone must examine his intention. For what and for whom is he working? For which purpose is he running from here to there? All of you must try to think about it. Everything that is not for the sake of the Lord is going to finish. Even if you spend millions of dollars, God knows everything. He knows that the Children of Adam in the twentieth century never follow His orders. No country is following the Orders of heavens, meaning the Orders of the Lord. Everyone is trying to make something according to his own thinking and his own knowledge. Much of what they are teaching in universities is nonsense, a majority of the subjects. Everything is only based on materialism. They deny all spirituality, everything beyond this world, and everything after this life.

Who never thinks about divine service, must be brought down. Even if he is the richest person on earth, it is not going to be of any benefit to him. Therefore, try to depend on the Lord Almighty. If you depend on Him and He supports you, no harm will come to you here or hereafter. But someone who is not following even the most simple commands of the religion should fall down, and be taken away quickly. One of those commands is to pray after ritual ablution[23], but people now have forgotten it.

In the third millennium, every satanic thing that they are using now should be taken away. Satan is making everything horrible and terrible for humankind. His teachings cause people to think wrongly, to intend wrongly, and to do wrong things.

Therefore, there is a divine trap for those who think that there will not be any heavenly involvement on earth any more, and who are saying, "We just threw away the kings and the sultans. Now we are the owners of everything which we took from them; it is for us, not for them any more."

One intention may save people, and one word may cause humankind to fall down, so that if people are not paying attention to their Lord's teachings and orders, everything is going to be upset, the head will be at the bottom, and the feet will be at the top. And everything may be taken from you, so that you are not able to taste anything from all those kinds of divine favors, *ni'mat,* like vegetables and fruits. You will ask to eat, but there will be no taste, nothing—eating the food, but nothing in your mouth is helping you to digest it.

Step-by-step, we are approaching the Divine Presence. Some people through their love and respect for the Lord Almighty even have a baby, to make Him happy and pleased with them. *Ask* in the new century for the best things, the best people from the Lord Almighty. Anything that you are asking for must be the best, the most expensive, the most valuable. Do not ask for straw like donkey-like people. But you may ask for a horse instead,

---

[23] It is a tradition, *sunnah,* of Prophet Muhammad ﷺ to pray two cycles of prayer, *rak'ats,* after making ablution, *wudu* or making the purificatory bath, *ghusl.*

and then the sultan may order, "Give that servant of the Lord Almighty from my treasures. Whatever he is asking for, give him double, and give something for his horse also."

So, if you depend on the Lord you should be successful here and Hereafter. If you are asking to depend on a man, then one day he is going to die and your pillar is falling down. If a person depends on his money, one day that money is going to vanish; it may even be lost in one night, and then he cannot do anything with it any more.

Ask from the Lord Almighty for a safe place for the coming days with good ones around you, so wild animals will not be able to touch you. You may keep yourself and the Lord Almighty is protecting you also.

May God forgive us and bless you. Unexpected events will soon begin to appear, and chaos is on the increase, day-by-day. May the Lord protect our souls, may He protect our families, our children, and make who is alive to be good servants. We are all servants, may Allah accept us. And from God is all success.[24] Fatiha.

Run to Find Your True Identity

There are going to be unexpected events, terrible, horrible, and fearful events, for which no one can bring an explanation. There are divine purposes and wisdom in those events. If one event is going to happen, after it there should be so many events coming immediately or suddenly. Up until today, so many expected events have come, but now and in the future, even if people are thinking about coming events, everything should be unexpected. This is a new beginning; a new period for this world is coming now.

From a very confused and complex life, people should come back to a very simple life, as it was before, at the beginning. Life has reached a top point, with countless burdens and efforts for mankind, who in the twentieth century reached to the height of its wishes. But suddenly a wave of unexpected power will come and remove everything that people have reached to during the last two-hundred years or more by science and technology—suddenly it all will vanish and disappear.

---

[24] Arabic: *wa min Allahi 't-tawfiq.*

Therefore, it is a time that people must try to get away from difficulties to a restful, comfortable, and simple life. The complex life now in our days is bringing countless difficulties, because modern science and its inventions are causing people to cut themselves off from nature. That break between humankind and nature makes people very strange outwardly, as well as in their inner life. Their appearance is ugly, and their inner thinking or understanding is unbalanced, useless, terrible.

This is a affliction from the Lord of the heavens because humankind separated, or ran away from nature, to an artificial life. Everything that surrounds people is artificial, and all artificial things are against nature. Nature never likes artificiality, and artificiality never likes nature. They are opposites. Now it is the end of a wild period, full of violence. The main creations of humankind that became rebellious against everything are science and technology. That is what is happening around the whole world now in our days, and a terrible end is waiting for the rebels.

Big events are coming to take away everything that makes humankind artificial. Technology has made people into artificial beings, and their genuine identity has left them. All of them are artificial. They are also using artificial means, so that they cannot do anything themselves anymore.

Therefore, we are saying that humankind should run back to nature now, to save itself and to find its true identity, because men and women lost their genuine identities. All of them are dressed in artificial identities.

Now, day-by-day, time is approaching an end that no one can prevent. Everything must run to its last point, its last station. The majority of people are going to vanish and finish because of unexpected events that should appear from East and West, from above and from below, causing people to pass on or lose their senses. People are not going to find what they need to eat and drink, and they are going to lose their physical being. People will try to save themselves in two ways: first, they will try to save their physical being, and second, they will try to reach to their spiritual reality. They must make a separation, so one side does not interfere in the other side, no. In addition, they must give each side what it needs.

Therefore, it is important now for everyone to try to be sometimes with their own true selves, because people have been taken away from their original identities. It is now a big obligation for you to ask to come back to your true personality, to find your identity. Man does not know who he is, if he is an animal or an angel. He is wondering, but he never finds out what his personality is, his identity. This is terrible and very dangerous.

You must try daily for some minutes to be with yourself, to come to yourself through meditation and contemplation, *muraqabah*. This is going to be a foundation for the life of humankind on earth in the third millennium.

Everyone must know what his true value is and must follow a new way after the destruction of humanities' qualities. Human beings, if they are not reaching in this very short period the special and valuable qualities that were granted to them by their Creator, are going to sink down. If they quickly run and find them, they are going to be saved. May Allah forgive us. Fatiha.

The Tunnel to Pass

What does the happiness or sadness of a human being depend on? It depends on whether he is obedient to the Lord's Divine Commands or not, respecting Him, or denying Him and following Satan.

All prophets have taught this and it is repeated at every congregational prayer sermon, *khutbatu 'l-Jumu'ah*, everywhere in the world to remind people, "O people, be obedient to the Lord, respect Him and fear Him, because He can see you everywhere. Wherever you are, you are under His Vision, *nazar*. Protect your heart; do not let evil enter in it. Among the creatures you have been given the highest rank, and God has chosen you for His Service, and that you may govern the world as His Deputies, according to His Divine ruling. However, you are throwing away this honor, and you want to make your own laws. What kind of Pharaohs have you become?"

The world is getting darker day by day. Now we are in the first month of the Islamic calendar, Muharram, and who knows what this coming year and later years will bring to us? We do not know what will happen, or if there will be many more years to come.

Our Lord is saying that He is giving the chance to rebellious human beings to remember Him, but people are misusing His generosity and make every bad thing even worse. The Holy Prophet ﷺ had been asking from the Lord Almighty that his Community, his *Ummah*, might not be punished like previous nations by something coming from the skies or from the earth. So the Lord Almighty said, "I will punish some of you through others of you."

We shall see so many trial this year and in the future. O people, you must understand the wisdom of your creation and existence. Life is short, death is waiting for us, the hereafter, *akhira*, is in front of us, and we will have to give an answer to the angels of the Grave.

It is as if the whole world is in a tunnel which looks like an X: it is getting narrower, and from a certain point it is getting wider, up to the eternal. Only spiritually strong people will pass through this tunnel. Materialist people will not be able to make it; the power of their batteries will be finished. Only the spiritual power of the soul can help you.

The Lord Almighty has ordered us to read the Holy Qur'an, to make *dhikr* and recite blessings on the Prophet ﷺ, *salawat,* to strengthen our souls and to connect to the spiritual world. But we do not understand; we are misunderstanding the religion. The orders and duties of religion, and particularly of Islam, are only for connecting you with the spiritual world. You have to know what worship is for.

Only because of your soul, which is coming from the "supersensible" world, *Malakut,* may you be called human beings. According to your physical body, you are animals. You must recognize your value. We should try to control our ego, *nafs*, but we are doing everything to please it, serving it.

You must try to shine with the light of your soul. This light has been granted to you from the heavens through the Holy Prophet ﷺ. Search for this light!

If not, so many things will happen in the near future. May Allah keep us on the path of Truth. Keep yourselves and learn to control your ego, so that you may be able to rise to the spiritual dimension, *Malakut.* Fatiha.

There Is No Compulsion in Religion

You cannot rule people by force. The Lord in His Wisdom is saying in the Holy Qur'an:

There is no compulsion (no force) in religion.[25]

Through this, God is saying, "Whoever wants to believe, may believe. Who does not want to believe, he does not have to believe. Both the believer and the unbeliever will return to Me. Do not force anyone to believe, because he will not really be a believer."

---

[25] Suratu 'l-Baqara, 2:256.

This is a big wisdom. In the twentieth century, they have tried to force people into so many things, but as soon as that the pressure was released, people returned to their old condition. It is the nature of humankind to be Muslim; you cannot separate it from that. As much as you try to paint over gold to cover it, still the gold remains under that paint. Keep this wisdom. The conscience is calling out, the inner feeling is guiding to goodness. Only the ego, *nafs*, is forcing us to evil, trying to paint us. Still there is that gold underneath.

Really, humankind is going on the straight path towards Allah. When babies make movements in the wombs of their mothers, they try to escape the angels that come according to the Lord's Command to make them to leave the womb. So the angels say to the Lord, "O our Lord, Your servant is disobedient, we cannot take him out." Then the manifestation of Divine spiritual power, *tajalli,* is descending on the baby, and it falls into prostration, *sajda*, coming out of the womb like that! At the end of our life, our soul will come to make prostration before its Lord again. Therefore, keep making *sajda* to the Lord Almighty. It is important! Without prostration there is danger that you may fall into the hands of Satan, making prostration to him instead.

Satanic Teachings

May the Lord Almighty take Satan far away from us. Those who get away from Satan—or who Satan is getting away from—are lucky people. There are no more troubles for them. Troubles exist only because of him. He is a first class troublemaker. As long as you accept him and follow him, there must be troubles for you. If you do not want to fall into troubles, if you would like your life to be safe here and Hereafter, do not follow Satan. Finished. It is so easy.

Satan is the number one enemy of humankind. He never likes you, but shows himself to you your advisor. He came to the first man Adam, and his lady Eve, and entered Paradise, where they were living in full enjoyment and safety, and full blessings were on them. What more could they ask? Satan came and said, "Come and follow me, I shall take you to a much more joyful place." When the first man and his lady followed him and took one step, a divine curse fell on them. Instead of enjoyment came sadness, instead of peace came fighting, instead of a restful and comfortable life came a life full of miseries and sufferings. Such is Satan's advice.

He always comes to people and says, "Come and follow me, I will take you to another, much better stage of life, and you may reach more comfort, enjoyment and happiness, more wealth and health." He is a liar. What can be better than Paradise?

When believers are passing from this life to everlasting life in Paradise, their enjoyments are increasing every day - not coming down and getting less and reaching zero, as in this world. In Paradise your enjoyment, respect, lights, knowledge and wisdom in the Divine Presence are always increasing, day-by-day through the Lord Almighty's blessings. He has endless favor oceans. Do you think He prepared those oceans for Himself? He is not in need of anything; He is God Almighty. He is creating, granting and giving these endless oceans of favors, Blessings and Mercy to you.

But Satan is coming and saying, "Come and follow me, I am taking you to the high life, for a perfect enjoyment without any limits. I will make you, my followers, to be happy." And ignorant people are asking, "How can there be a perfect enjoyment?" And he says, "Look at what I did: I refused to obey my Lord, and then He granted me my freedom. Now I am free from obedience, worship, prayer, and glorification. Only once I was disobedient, and now I am free and I do as I like. No one is calling me to come and pray and fast, no one is telling me to do this or that. O people, follow me."

Therefore, freedom is passing through disobedience. Satan's teaching to people is, "O people, you must try to be free. The way to freedom is passing through disobedience, so do not follow anyone, but follow me. I am not telling you to obey me, no, because we are fighting obedience. But I am only advising you with a sweet word: follow me. O Europeans, Americans, anyone, I am not telling you to obey me, no, it is very heavy. I refused it, and now I have my own will, doing everything I want, and no one is questioning me: What are you doing or not doing? Perfect willpower is with me."

"I rely solely on Allah, and His Blessings and Protection."[26] Satan's teaching of freedom, to be free from heavenly commands, has taken away the minds of people in the twenty-first century. They are asking for that freedom. He is advising them, "You are living on earth. Do not obey what is coming to you from the heavens, telling you to do this and not to do that."

---

[26] Arabic: *Hasbi Allahu wa ni'mal wakeel.*

After that, people were coming and inventing new rights, granting you freedom, or better, declaring freedom and ordering it to you, because they first declare that humanity is created free and must be free throughout its whole life, and no one can prevent its freedom. In what way free? That is satanic teaching. Therefore, youngsters are saying now, "We do not need to follow heavenly commands. We must be free so we can use our free will as we like."

The second satanic teaching is saying, "You must fight, as you fought heavenly teachings before, and be disobedient instead of obedient servants. Do not say 'servants', you are not servants. You are 'Number One,' most important people, all of you are VIPs. How may a VIP be a servant, what is that?" They are very happy, saying, "Disobedience is our honor."

Satan is saying, "You must be free from heavenly commands, not to be servants. Be disobedient. When you are going to be disobedient, they will not call you a servant, no. Then you have reached my level. I am not a servant. I am the king of disobedient people, and they are my supreme staff. I am sitting with them, getting up with them. I am always with them, because they are chosen ones, elected ones. Occasionally we have elections also, to elect someone who is much closer to my satanic presence, like Trotsky, Mao, Mussolini, Hitler, this or that one, who are elected as my staff. I trained them like a trainer of a football team, how to be against servanthood. And the twenty-first century is under my hegemony, my kingdom is just established."

A'udhu billah.[27] I am asking for divine protection from the Lord Almighty. If He is not sheltering us, nobody can. I hope that these satanic tricks and traps are going to finish, that his authority will break down, and that in the third millennium servanthood of heavens will appear in the East and West. May Allah bless you and make everyone try to be a good servant for our Lord's divine service.

On the first day of this year everything changed suddenly. Spirituality is increasing, and materialism is going down. We are anticipating the time for Satan's sultanate to come down. Thanks O our Lord, *Shukr, ya Rabbi.* Fatiha.

---

[27] "I seek refuge in God from evil."

Good Manners Are the Soul of Knowledge

Do not look down upon anything or anyone. The ego only loves itself. It is *kafir*, not accepting Allah, and it wants to be sitting alone on the Throne. The Holy Prophet ﷺ said, "God Himself has taught me the best manners, *adab*."[28]

A human being is living through his soul, and the soul of knowledge is *adab*. Knowledge without *adab* is a misfortune for its owner. Satan had knowledge, but he had no *adab*, behaving badly in God's Presence, and then he was finished. Always the ego is bad mannered, going against Allah, denying Him. It never likes to be under the control of anyone. All our egos are the same. We have to bring it under control, and train it to become our Lord's servant, and not be controlled by the ego.

Our Lord is not forcing anyone. Not everybody can keep his ego, and they are falling from one trouble into the next, never finding any rest or peace.

Man needs, and must learn good manners, *adab*. It is not easy to teach *adab*. Someone may read hundreds or thousands of books, but he may not be able to control his ego. He may have knowledge, but he cannot practice it. Satan had so much knowledge, and it did not benefit him. And everybody in our time wants to study, and they all fail the test.

And someone may go on pilgrimage, *Hajj*; he may stay forty days, make *Hajj*, *Umrah*, visit the Prophet ﷺ, *Ziyarah*, and become clean. Everything seems perfect. But then he gets on the plane home and he looks to a flight attendant with desire, and everything is lost, finished. Six months, one year he stayed there, so many prayers he did, *tawafs*, *Umrahs*, everything is good. But then, for one moment he does not control his ego, forgetting that God is looking to him, forgetting and being without God, and Satan makes him forget.

Do not give a chance to Satan, because he is always looking for an opportunity to catch people. There is the forbidden, *haram*, and permissible, *halal*. Whoever is not respecting that border falls out of good conduct, *adab*, with the Lord. Few people want to save themselves from their bad-mannered ego. *Sufi orders* and the four schools of law, *madhabs*, are based on

---

[28] Ibn as-Sama'nee in his *Adab al-mala'*. Ibn Jawzi and Imam Suyuti authenticated it.

good conduct, *adab*, and that is why Satan is against them, because they are against his school. His school is the fifth, the school of wrongdoing and falsehood, *batil*. So many people follow it. May our Lord not leave us in the hands of our bad ego. Whoever is not asking that will be caught by Satan.

Your ego is telling you that you are number one; that nobody is like you. It is telling you that you do not have to listen to anyone, that you are strong and know everything, that you are your own shaykh. And the ego is lying to us.

What we are saying here is what they have put in our hearts, and we are ashamed in front of God and fearing Him because we are such ignorant ones, making so many mistakes and bad-mannered actions. Who is the shaykh? He is that one who teaches you about God and His Prophet ﷺ. How you can know by yourself? But they do not want to accept a teacher, and whoever does not accept a shaykh, an *imam*, a guide, his teacher is Satan. He is telling them, "Why do you need a shaykh?"

Follow a pure guide that he may take you to purity, because only pure ones will enter Paradise. God knows best who are the hypocrites. We are trying, working on it, asking to be clean.

Those who believe, then disbelieve, then believe again and then again disbelieve.[29]

Sometimes we believe and sometimes not, listening to our ego and Satan. On the way of faith, *iman*, you can be saved.

And the angels of the Grave will ask you if your face is turned towards the worldly life, *dunya*, or towards the Lord, Allah. They will ask you what is your *qiblah*, to where is your heart directed? If they find your face turned towards the Lord, everything is good. But if they find your face turned away from Him, then God will also turn away from you. If in prayer you turn your eyes away from the place of *sajda*, looking left and right three times, then God is saying, "My servant has turned away from Me. Leave him." This is an important point in manners. Do not behave badly in the Presence of the Sultan.

May our Lord forgive us and not throw us out of the Community of Prophet Muhammad ﷺ. Fatiha.

---

[29] Suratu 'n-Nisa, 4:137.

To Me My Own Faith, and to You Yours

You have to protect yourself against your enemies. In our time they are saying truth is falsehood, and falsehood is truth. There is such ignorance, and it is now the second period of ignorance, *jahiliyya*. The first period was before the arrival of the Prophet Muhammad ﷺ. Do not occupy yourself with ignorant, square-headed people who never understand anything, even learned people who confuse wrong with right. They are saying, "What is the difference? A pilgrim is going to greet and kiss the Black Stone, saying God is the Greatest; what is he hoping for from that, and we are saluting in front of a black statue?"

They become demagogues comparing things that cannot be compared. Therefore, say to them *"to you your belief, and to me my belief."*[30] Do not dispute with them, as it will only weaken your faith. Our time is like that now.

The Holy Prophet ﷺ said:

> A time will come to my Community when your leaders will make you happy and you will run to please them, and another time will come when your leaders will be so ugly.[31]

This refers to men and women without any lights on their faces, because they turned away from God.

When you look into the mirror, you must be thankful if God gave you excellent manners. Ask Him not to make you ugly so that people turn away from you. Whose face is turned towards the Lord, who is making prostration, sajda, cannot be ugly. But who has turned away from Him and who is not worshipping the Lord will become ugly. Open the graves and look how their faces are.

I repent and return to God. My Lord, increase our light! O our Lord, increase our lights, O Light of Light! [32] Pray for lights from God. Lights cannot be burned by fire, or lamps would not shine. But light, *nur*, is governing fire.

---

[30] Suratu 'l-Kafirun, 109:6.

[31] Tirmidhi.

[32] Arabic: *Tubtu wa rajatu ila'llah. Rabbi, zidna Nuran. Ya Nur an-Nur.*

Why are unbelievers seeing believers as ugly? Once Sayyidina Abu Bakr ♦ came to the Prophet ﷺ and at the same time came Abu Jahl, the biggest enemy of the Prophet ﷺ. Sayyidina Abu Bakr ♦ said, "O Prophet of God, my spirit and soul are at your feet. You are the most beautiful person I ever saw."

"You are right, Abu Bakr."

But Abu Jahl said, "Oh no, you are the most ugly one."

"You are also right, Abu Jahl."

The Companions of the Prophet ﷺ were surprised. "How can both of them be right?"

And the Prophet ﷺ said, "Because I am like a mirror; Abu Bakr saw his own beauty in it and Abu Jahl his own ugliness."

A true believer cannot be ugly; that is for those who have no belief.

3. News for the Future of Humankind

Springtime for Faith

Trees that are losing their leaves in winter, even if you put water or fertilizer on them, will not get green at that time because it is not the season.

What God has planted, it will not die. They are thinking that faith is finished, that the Holy Prophet ﷺ was an ordinary person. It is winter for faith now, and they are thinking that everything green is finished, but the seasons are changing, and when the winter is finished, the green comes out of the earth again. What has been sleeping under the earth according to God's order will come up. Even if they should try to prevent this happening, it is not possible. It is nature's law, and after the first snow falls, more and more flowers will appear. So no matter how much they are shouting and making bad things and laws against faith now, the time has come. The spring of faith cannot be prevented.

And they are wondering: Who is doing that, how it is happening? Yes, look for that One and find Him. Fatiha.

Useless Technology

The twentieth century was fertile planting ground for everything, including good or bad ideas. And in the beginning, what is coming out of the ground is all looking the same; no one can know if that plant is just grass or a tree.

But with the arrival of the twenty-first century, all false ideas, all teachings of Satan, have begun to dry and die, like grass in the summer sun, while trees are standing up with greatness and continuing to grow.

Therefore, now, they are cheating people with so many foolish ideas that look like the others. But do not occupy yourself with them. Wait and look, what is going to happen.

We are worrying now about what is going to happen, and it is going to be a big change, because all nations, humankind, the Children of Adam, are trusting and depending on technology. It is for them like the main pillar that keeps the roof of their house up. The main pillar of the whole world is technology, and that pillar is going to fall, or collapse on itself, and the roof, the whole building, is going to fall down.

This is important to know. And you can imagine what is going to happen when technology is finished. It means that everything that you now call civilization is going to finish. The whole civilization of the western countries, who are so proud with their technology, should fall very badly when technology dies, when that pillar, which is keeping their civilization up, is destroyed.

You will not be able to move one step outside your home to bring something or to take something away; you will not be able to use electricity, you will not be able to use water.

And these high buildings... who can fly six floors, ten floors, twenty, eighty, one hundred floors up? You must begin in the morning to reach up there in the evening. And it will be dark; you cannot see who is facing you on the stairs. No security, no safety. The chaos which is coming after that mindless technology is terrible, horrible. Millions are going to pass on. Where can they go? It is the middle of winter, the whole world is frozen, and no one can reach from one place to another easily. Where are you going to go? What are you going to do? No water reaching up, no electricity, no fire.

I am thinking that here in Turkish Cyprus our houses are so simple; there is no need for an elevator. But, foolishly, in the towns they began to build high buildings, from concrete; they are like an oven in summer and in winter like a refrigerator. How can you live like that? And people cannot move three steps without their car, but cars will not be able to move; how will they go from one place to another? People are accustomed to live by pressing buttons. And water, that it is coming from three hundred to four hundred feet down, how will it come up? No electricity.

Therefore, I am looking to move to places, where water is going to be nearby for using and drinking. The countryside everywhere is much safer and it is clean.

Run Back to Nature

Man now is forced to come back to nature. Twentieth-century civilization made him run away from nature, fighting it, harming it with such foolish factories, wasting supplies, foolishly. Now the Lord is chastising humankind. Enough! Oceans have died, what is that? For what? For quick wasting of everything. That is the base of economics: fast supply, fast wasting. No more can nature supply foolish humankind now. Therefore, the Lord Almighty is going to chastise them, so that people should save even one cup of water, and not waste it. This is coming in our time. To wash one cup they are opening the tap and wasting half a gallon of water. They must learn.

You must apply this point to everything: do not waste anything. You must learn and try to come back to nature, so that nature is not fighting you. As much as you are fighting nature, nature is fighting you back. When you make peace with nature, nature will help you in your life. Then fatal diseases for which they claim to have no cure will disappear.

Look at crowded cities everywhere. It will be impossible to live in them in the third millennium. People must go out to the countryside, dig wells and use them. And you must not throw away the fat of animals, because from it will be made candles. No more electricity; you cannot use lamps any more, no paraffin. Only flashlights, as before, burning and giving light. And fireplaces should be used for cooking and heating inside. You are going to wear and use your clothes much longer, not putting on a new dress every day or every week. Industry will be finished. You must think about it. This is important for everyone. If not, so many people are going to pass on.

Even now, when sometimes they cut the electricity here for two hours or even only one hour, people go crazy. What about when it is cut for days and there is no hope for it to come back? If it is only cut for one hour, we may have hope that it will finish, that it will be reconnected and come back. But at that time, there will be no more hope for that power to come back again, finished. That is terrible. You will not be able to use anything. People, who live their lives on computers, TV, radio, are going to pass away because they will have no more hope for coming days.

We have hope, we are believers; we know that this is only a bridge from one side to another. Materialism is going to finish, and we are passing on a bridge to another point of life. Who is reaching that second life of this world should find that another source of power is coming into action. Therefore, we are not hopeless, but hopeful! Only for a short distance you must pay attention, so that you may pass freely through that valley.

Everything depends on beliefs. Who does not believe, you cannot make them believe. If they believe in spirituality through Islam, that will be useful for them. If they are materialist people, depending on material life and technology only, we will not use it on the other side, so there is no hope for them.

You are asking about your family and friends; they should carry many more difficulties in their life. My advice is to go to the countryside, where it is going to be more safe. Crowded places, cities, are going to be more dangerous. You must have a well because life depends on water. Without water, there is no life. Keep some animals, so that you may feed yourself with them. Live in simple houses. Try to come to a simple, natural life, not using TV and any of those technological instruments, because they are going to finish. You must keep everything with care, so that you do not waste what you have. Whoever wastes is going to finish.

When you are in the countryside, you do not have to stay in the house all day. You may move around, as Allah is ordering us to do. Do not go to big cities, there are so many problems there: robbers, countless Satanic groups. Everyone who is entering their places and closes the door with *Bismillahi 'r-Rahmani 'r-Rahim*—*"in the name of God, the Compassionate, the Merciful,"* should be protected.

There is a Tradition of the Prophet Muhammad ﷺ, *hadith*, that there will come a time when the sun will rise from the West, come up to the midday place and set, as it was rising, so that for three days there will be no sunshine. That will be the last point for people to repent, the last door, and then it will be closed.

May our Lord forgive us and bless you. Fatiha.

The Coming of the Anti-Christ

Do not think that the fire of war is going to stop: it will grow. For the whole world, it is going to be difficult.

The Holy Prophet ﷺ has said:

> When that fire is going around the whole world, and safety will be only in the Middle East area of Sham.[33]

[33] Tabarani.

Armageddon, it will be so difficult, and billions of people are going to pass on. Any time that you may find a way, go to Sham.

The north of Europe, Arctic Circle, Norway, are going to be safer than the south, but fire should be in the middle of the continent. Safe places will be in western Norway, Sham, southern Chile, southern Argentina, and places where there are no military bases.

Stay in the countryside, until Sayyidina Mahdi ﷺ stands up and calls people to come to Sham. Then you may run there because the Anti-Christ will appear and go around the world, making big tribulations; making people to lose faith or killing them. You may stay in your house in the countryside, keep yourself there and do not come out when you hear the armies of the Anti-Christ passing. Take ablution, close the doors, say, *Bismillahi 'r-Rahmani 'r-Rahim—"in the name of God, the Compassionate, the Merciful,"* and sit inside until his armies pass by, and then you should be in safety.

But now so many people will suffer divine chastisement, because they are opposing the Lord of the heavens. Most people are going to be unbelievers.

Be true and do not be afraid. Be pitiful and compassionate towards all creatures and you should be sheltered. And there is no shelter except with the Lord. Do not trust in money, not even in gold. But keep food for yourself for at least one, two, or three months. In three months everything is going to be clear. But those chastisement should come from the skies, affecting so many countries and taking away so many people, like the flood in the time of Noah ﷺ. That was a flood of water, but this is fire now, carrying everything away.

Only when Sayyidina Mahdi ﷺ is saying "God is Greatest!" *Allahu Akbar*, three times, the war is going to stop. Who is asking to be sheltered must pray, make prostration, *sajda,* have no bad intentions and must not do cruelties, *dhulm.* Who is cruel, must be taken away. Do not have bad actions, bad thoughts or bad intentions against anyone. Such people will be taken away. Therefore, from seven people, only one may remain on earth.

You must take care to be true and trustworthy ones, to be trustworthy, *amin,* so that you may meet Sayyidina Mahdi ﷺ. Keep to yourself, and ask shelter from the Lord Almighty: there is no shelter except with Him.

As God states in Holy Qur'an:

We have honored the Children of Adam.[34]

Do not let yourself be swept away like garbage. Honor is believing in the Lord Almighty. Try to reach people with the light of Islam, to guide them out of their darkness to Divine lights. Fatiha.

Return to Nature

When Grandshaykh said that technology is going to finish, no one believed him. But now scientists and computer specialists are speaking about it. Computers are going to finish, and all those technical inventions, that were intended to make the life of Man easier, really made our powers to come down to zero, because everything that we did before with physical power is done by machines now. The Lord Almighty is bringing an end to that period, and everything must have an end.

My advice to my followers is to come back to nature, and to begin to put into action, and to practice, their own physical powers, not to give commands to machines to do this and not to do that. Step-by-step, we must try to save our freedom from technology, to bring ourselves to ourselves. It is important what we are saying now. You must try not to use these machines and instruments. Use them less and less. When the electricity is suddenly cut, many many people may pass on. Who did not prepare himself for a new period should pass suddenly or go crazy. Depression, a very bad depression should come to people, which is impossible to treat, because medicine will be expired. Factories and everything are going to stop. No more will doctors cut people, no more operations, no more caesarians.

Step-by-step, try to come back to your natural position and to use manpower. Learn how to live without technology and how to act by yourself. Be alert! Do not build high buildings; make them only two floors. Do not use concrete, cement, iron, but use mud, timber, stones. Use wells, because there will be no more running water. No more electricity, cars, telephones.

---

[34] Suratu 'l-Isra, 17:70.

Now, until Sayyidina Mahdi ﷺ is coming, there will be a period of three to six months when so many things happen. People are going to go lose their minds, harm themselves or pass on, so that from seven people only one will remain. Who is depending on technology, is going to be in trouble. In only one night, from evening until the morning, huge numbers of people may pass on. In every country there should be safe areas between two countries, passages that no one is using. Go according to your inspiration. The first sign is for water to be near - five, ten, fifteen meters.

Believers should be in safety, worshippers much more, and servants for the Lord's Divine Presence should be in full safety.

When the Anti-Christ is coming, there should be an opening for you to come quickly to Sham. For forty days every believer must be there, and then the Anti-Christ should be defeated by Jesus Christ, 'Isa ﷺ. Then the whole world should be open, peaceful and safe.

When Mahdi ﷺ is coming, at that time another power will open, so that no one is going to ask for technology. The Lord Almighty is going to grant to common people the power of Islam—miraculous powers, like those He previously granted to His prophets and saints. You will not need to fly, but you will move with instant steps. You will look from here to that horizon, and by reciting *Bismillahi 'r-Rahmani 'r-Rahim – "in the name of God, the Compassionate, the Merciful,"* as far as your eye is reaching, you may put your foot there.

Since 1940, I have been waiting for that day. There was one Grandshaykh in Istanbul who was saying, "I can foresee that spring is coming, and Last Days approach with its tribulations, followed by the appearance Mahdi ﷺ." They were expecting Mahdi ﷺ and Jesus Christ ﷺ to come at that time. They will appear soon, God-willing, and we hope to be with them. Fatiha.

Heavenly Blessings of Muharram

Bismillahi 'r-Rahmani 'r-Rahim—"in the name of God, the Compassionate, the Merciful." It is one of holiest months, Muharram, and tonight is the tenth, one of holiest nights in Islam. Tomorrow is the tenth of Muharram, the

Ashura day[35]. It has a very special place in the Islamic calendar, and also in the calendar of worldwide historical events, because on this day the Lord Almighty granted victory to His beloved servants from His endless mercy oceans, and from His endless power oceans. On this day:

- God accepted the repentance of Prophet Adam ﷺ after he was thrown out from Paradise.
- The Ark of Prophet Noah ﷺ landed on the peak of that mountain and the flood just finished.
- Prophet Abraham ﷺ was saved from the fire of Nimrod.
- Prophet Joseph ﷺ was brought back with his father Jacob ﷺ.
- Prophet Moses ﷺ passed through the Red Sea and was saved from Pharaoh.
- God spoke directly to Prophet Moses ﷺ and gave him the Commandments.
- Prophet Jonah ﷺ was saved from the stomach of the whale.
- Prophet David ﷺ was forgiven.
- Prophet Solomon the King ﷺ, was granted the kingdom over all humankind and jinn.
- Prophet Job ﷺ became healthy, and more wealthy than before.
- Prophet Jesus Christ ﷺ was taken up to the heavens.
- Prophet Muhammad ﷺ was granted much honor and an opening of the seven heavens for himself and for his whole nation, and he was saved from his tribe, the Quraysh.
- Prophet Muhammad's ﷺ grandson, Husayn ؓ, achieved the honor of martyrdom when he was killed by an oppressor's army.

And every time that Muslims fell into difficulties, divine help and support just reached them through this holy month, and particularly on a day like tomorrow, on the tenth of Muharram. Very important.

I was hoping Sayyidina Mahdi ﷺ to come in the twentieth century, but yet some signs have not been completed. And I hope that he may be with us soon, after the year 2000. The third millennium should be for Mahdi ﷺ.

---

[35] In Islam, the day begins at sunset.

So many heavenly blessings reached to believers on the tenth of Muharram, and it is good luck to reach to Muharram. And I hope that it is going to be granted for Sayyidina Mahdi ☶ to appear soon. Tonight, much more power should be granted, perhaps the authority for the whole world. And his sword, now, is taken out a little bit. Tonight it is going to appear.

And, as we said before, one month ago in *Dhu 'l-Hijjah* on the night of Arafat, a change began. There is a new a Divine Appearance, *tajalli*, a new power that will continue now without stopping. Miraculous powers from tonight are beginning to come into action step-by-step, so that when technology is going to finish and vanish, another kind of power is going to be ready for use.

Try to be with the Lord and you are going to be victorious. Try to take yourself, step-by-step, away from the hands of Satan and devils. Try to use less of every kind of instrument that Satan and his soldiers helped to invent, because everything that is working with electricity is going to stop, and another source of power is beginning to act.

At some point, for a few months only, all nations are going to carry very heavy burdens. When that finishes, there will be a new opening for the whole world. No need at that time for electricity, cars, ships, factories. No. The light of your faith, *Nur al-iman*, is going to surround you. Your body is shining, so that even in the darkness of the night you may go.

Therefore, I am happy and thankful to Allah that we have reached to this night and we are asking humbly for our names to be written with Mahdi ☶. We are not happy with the situation in the world, East and West, because every system, all living systems on earth now, are against the divine rules and laws.

We are happy and proud enough that the Lord Almighty makes us happy with Him, with His saints, *awliya*, with *Sahibu 'z-Zaman* Sayyidina Mahdi ☶, not to run after that satanic, dirty life. Satanic life is the dirtiest. Run away from the dirty life. If not, you may sink in those dirty waters, dirty situations, and you cannot save yourself. Ask for cleanliness and try to be clean, so that you should be clean in the last moment of your life. Fatiha.

The Significance Of Ashura

Alhamdulillah, all praise is to God, Who has blessed us to see another year. The first month of this year is Muharram. In this month is an excellent day, the day of Ashura, which falls on the tenth of Muharram. The Holy Prophet ﷺ recommended that we fast on this day, according to his practice, *sunnah*. He also indicated how we should observe the fast of Ashura.

The Holy Prophet ﷺ arrived in Madinah and found the Jews observing fast on the day of Ashura. They said, "It is the day of great (significance) when God delivered Moses عليه السلام and his people, and drowned Pharaoh and his people. Sayyidina Moses عليه السلام observed fast out of gratitude, and we also observe it." So God's Messenger ﷺ observed fast (on the day of Ashura) and gave us orders to observe it."[36]

The Prophet ﷺ said:

It is the day of Ashura. God has not made fasting obligatory for you, but I am fasting. He who likes to observe fast among you should do so, and he who likes not to observe it (does not have to).[37]

The Holy Prophet ﷺ said:

The fast on the tenth of Muharram atones for the sins of the preceding year.[38]

The Holy Prophet ﷺ said:

After Ramadan, the fasts of Muharram have the greatest excellence. [39]

The Holy Prophet ﷺ said:

If I survive till next year, I will definitely observe fast on the ninth of Muharram (as well).[40]

The Holy Prophet ﷺ meant that he would also fast on the ninth as well as the tenth, to which he was accustomed. We also should try fasting on the ninth and the tenth of Muharram.

Worship the Lord as much as you can on Ashura, as:

---

[36] *Sahih Bukhari* and *Muslim*.
[37] *Sahih Muslim*.
[38] *Sahih Muslim*.
[39] *Sahih Muslim*.
[40] *Sahih Muslim*.

- Whoever fasts on this day is like one who fasts all his life.
- Whoever clothes a naked person, God will release him from a painful chastisement.
- He who visits a sick person, God will grant him a reward that will not be decreased.
- Whoever places his hand on an orphan's head, or feeds a hungry person or gives water to a thirsty man, God will feed him a feast from
- Paradise and will quench his thirst with *salsabeel* (a wine that does not intoxicate).
- Whoever takes full bath of purification, *ghusl,* on this day will enjoy excellent health and freedom from sickness and indolence.
- Whoever provides generously for his family on this day, God will be generous to him throughout this year.
- Whoever applies kohl to his eyes will never suffer from eye pain again, God -willing.

O our Lord! Bless us to perform good deeds and gain their reward on Ashura. Make the New Year one of unity, cooperation, and success for Muslims in this city and around the world. *Ameen.*

Instructions for Worship on Ashura

Between the noon prayer *(Dhuhr)* and the afternoon prayer (*'Asr*): Pray four cycles *(rakaats)*, reciting in each:

1 time Sūratu 'l-Fātiḥa
10 times Sūratu 'l-Ikhlāṣ

Recite the following *dhikr*:

1000 times *lā ilāha ill-Allāh*

There is none to be worshipped but God.

1000 times ṣalawāt: *Allāhumma ṣalli 'alā Muḥammadin wa 'alā āli Muḥammadin wa sallim.*

O our Lord, exalt Muhammad and the family of Muhammad and grant them peace.

1000 times Sūratu 'l-Ikhlāṣ

Invoke God with the following prayer:

Allāhumma thabitnā ʿala 'l-ḥaqq,

O our Lord, make us steadfast in the way of Reality,

Yā Ghāliban ghaira maghlūb,

O Victorious One, never defeated,

Yā Nāṣira 'l-mu'minīn,

O Support of the believers,

Yā Ghiyātha 'l-mustaghīthīn,

O Succour of those seeking rescue,

Yā Qarīban ghaira bāʿid,

O Near One, never far,

Yā Shāhidan ghaira mashhūd.

O Present One, never absent,

Ḥasbī-Allāhu wa niʿm al-wakīl

God is sufficient for us and the Most generous of appointees

Lā ḥawla wa lā quwwata illa billāhi 'l-ʿAlīyyi 'l-ʿAẓīm.

There is no power and no might except with God the most High, the Tremendous.

Ghufrānaka, Rabbanā, wa ilayka 'l-maṣīr.

Your forgiveness for us, we beseech, O our Lord and to Thee is the return.

Rabbanā taqabbal-minnā, Bi ḥurmati'l-ḥabīb. Fātiḥa.

O our Lord accept from us for the sake of the Beloved. Fātiḥa.

Keep Islam's Originality

Shukr ya Rabbi, shukr alhamdulillah, tawbah ya Rabbi, astaghfirullah. Thanks to my Lord, thanks and all praise are due to You; I turn to you my Lord, seeking forgiveness O God.

We are thanking the Lord Almighty, that we have reached the last Muharram of the second millennium, and the last Ashura, the tenth day of

Muharram, before the year 2000. Who knows if soon we are going to be with Mahdi ؏? Allah knows. We are looking and waiting for the time when Mahdi ؏ comes.

All the prophets and their communities respected this holy day by fasting. The Holy Prophet said:

If I reach next year, I am going to fast on this day.

Jewish people were fasting on Ashura for one day. To honor Ashura, to honor Prophet Moses ؏ and the salvation of the Children of Israel, Muslims fast two days: either on the ninth and tenth, or on the ninth, tenth and eleventh.

Now Muslims are leaving the originality of Islam. If you have a chance to be in the Divine Presence, do not lose it. Islam is number one. We have full honor and respect in the Divine Presence, and we have fully original rules.

But now people are accepting to be number one million, not number one, two or three, and that is the characteristic of our ego. The ego is representing full laziness. Nobody can surpass our ego's laziness. Therefore, we are saying, "Does not matter, it is okay for us, no need to be number one, and to be glorious. It is enough; we are happy to be the last number, so that no one is after us, no one is following us, and we are free to be the sultans of the lazy ones."

That is the opinion of our ego, and to say that is bringing Muslims dishonor; there is no more honor for them. Twentieth century Muslims never follow the rules of Islam because if they did they would be number one.

But they are saying, "We are very humble people, to be the last ones instead of the first ones."

And the Lord Almighty is making them to be dishonored. Imitation people in Islam now are very happy to follow western customs.

The Holy Prophet ﷺ indicated that you must follow the Islamic way. But people now run after western countries, leaving the *Shari'ah* and asking their governments to be westernized. They never like to be number one Muslims, always asking to be the last ones, preferring the non-Muslim world. They are thinking that if they are not westernized, western governments and nations are never going to accept them. Yes, it is true, but Allah may accept you.

Muslim nations throw away that honor and say, "We prefer our honor to be through western countries, not in the Divine Presence."

May Allah forgive us and bless you. We are asking for a true one to be the sultan on earth, and for us to be with him. Fatiha.

4. Islam Is Original and Spiritual

Heavenly Religions Embody Spirituality

Every calendar is based on a holy event. The Christian calendar is for the remembrance of Jesus Christ's birthday, and the Islamic calendar is based on the *Hijra* (the holy migration of the Prophet from Makkah to Madinah). That means that everything is founded on heavenly events or commands. The date of the birth of Jesus Christ is not really clear; people say this or that. It does not matter. What's important is, that calendar is based on his birthday, and that he was a heavenly being, a messenger from the heavens, sent to the Children of Israel.

You may ask, "What about other nations?" Yes, at the same time, the Lord Almighty sent local prophets to them from among themselves, to show them their way to the heavens. No doubt, there was not such a big population on earth at that time; the world was empty.

All the prophets were calling their nations to their Lord, not to *dunya*. There is no need for people to have prophets to teach them earthly purposes. No. Everyone knows very well the ways of this life, what it needs. But all prophets came to save people from the hands of their egos and to call them to the Lord Almighty's divine service, because people were running to satanic service, as they are now. No longer do people take any interest in the heavenly, divine service; they are only running after this life's purposes, for the service of this life.

Sayyidina Moses ﷺ had been sent to call the Children of Israel to Allah. They were the most important nation that the Lord Almighty had chosen. But some left his heavenly teachings, becoming disobedient and fighting him. The Lord Almighty had ordered them through Moses to accept His holy commands.

Spirituality is the main pillar of every religion. Without it, there is no meaning for a religion. If there is no spirituality, it is only going to be a kind of school of thought, like a school of philosophy. They are thinking and making arrangements, and call people to accept that, but there is no spirituality in that, never. That is the only difference, that heavenly religions have spirituality. But manmade religions, mind productions, never ask for it, there is no room for spirituality in their beliefs. They say, "We are accepting only what we can see, hear, and touch. Beyond that, we are never accepting."

Then the Lord Almighty sent Jesus Christ 🕊 whose creation was extraordinary, miraculous. Miracles all belong to spirituality, because the material power that we have cannot do what spiritual power can do. the Lord Almighty sent Jesus in a miraculous way through his mother, and no man had ever touched her. That story about the carpenter, Joseph, has no reality, *astaghfirullah!*[41] She, peace be upon her, was pure, clean. It was fully a miracle, a miraculous event for a baby to be born without a father. People were running around saying, "How it can be?"

One thousand years had passed since the time of Prophet Moses 🕊, and most of his miracles had been forgotten. How was he saved, and how did he destroy the sultanate of Pharaoh? Was it an ordinary thing? Was it not a miracle? But materialistic people will never learn.

On the order of the Lord Almighty, Prophet Moses 🕊 took seventy representatives to a meeting with Him. They were made to hear what Prophet Moses 🕊 was speaking about with Allah. And what did they say finally? "O Moses, show us who was speaking to you." They did not believe. That is the principle of materialism.

There is a group of materialistic people in Islam—the Wahabis. They never accept any miracles and spirituality in our belief. If you speak about it, they are saying, "You are idol worshippers, *mushrik.*" Terrible!

After the Prophet Moses, the Lord Almighty sent Jesus Christ in a miraculous way so people would accept the power of the Lord. At least they should have learned from all those miracles that if the Lord Almighty is asking to do something, He is only going to say, "Be," and that thing is going to happen.

That is the power of the Lord Almighty. Miracles are nothing. He may say to all the universes, "Come in appearance," and all of them will come. He may say, "Go away from existence," and all of them will just disappear and vanish. Allah is Almighty!

---

[41] "I seek refuge in Allah."

The Lord Almighty was only calling people from materialism to spirituality. Materialism is just against spirituality, and every religion must have spirituality; without it no religion can stand or continue. It is only spirituality, genuine spirituality, which makes Islam to reach up to today. If not for this, it would have finished.

May Allah forgive us and bless you. Fatiha.

The Firmly-rooted Faith

Satan is on full alert to take faith away, and yet faith is growing. Is it possible that humankind can take away the Himalayan Mountains? Or do you think that humankind can stop the moon from moving, or the sun from rising or setting? Never. And yet that might be possible, perhaps. But to remove Islam, that is impossible. Since fifteen centuries ago, people have been trying to take away even a little bit, yet the faith is standing up.

Everything may be changed, but Islam is never going to be changed. Satan tried his luck to change the book of Prophet Moses ﷺ, the Old Testament, the Torah. And if humankind puts his hand on a holy book to change it, that book immediately loses its sacredness, and its holiness is finished. Holy books are all virgin. When humans alter them, the virginity of those books just vanishes.

Satan came to Islam also, trying to change the Holy Qur'an. But it cannot be. The Lord the Lord Almighty said, "I am sending it, and I am looking after it, finished. No one can put his hand on it to change even one letter. I am the Guardian and Protector; I am the Supreme Keeper of that Book. It is one and the same Book from East to West, from North to South." the Lord Almighty is always victorious. Whoever is going to be with Him is also victorious. Whoever is with Satan is always defeated, going down, down, down, and finishing.

Only those who are with the Lord the Lord Almighty will stand up; others will fall down. And Satan is going to be like a donkey. Every *batil* (falsehood) that he has brought, the opposite of *haqq* (truth) and every fault that he did up today, and that he has urged and encouraged people to do, teaching them through technology, will be loaded on him to be taken away. Finished. Time is over, and we are counting down now. All *batil* will be loaded on Satan to be taken away to Hell (*jahannam*) when Jesus Christ comes.

May Allah grant us genuine faith to believe in such things. Islam is not just a set of rules for this life, measures for this material life; Islam has spirituality. What we are speaking about, the spirituality of Islam, is something that the Wahabis, Salafis and other materialistic people in Islam are denying. They are denying *tasawwuf,* Sufi ways, and any spirituality in any religion, and particularly in Islam. They are only interested in material measures, in the material life and its arrangements, taking only that, and leaving the spirituality of Islam. If you speak about spirituality, they accuse you, "You are a Sufi, and Sufis are *mushriks*... you are making people worship shaykhs, and prophets." They are such foolish, square head, mindless people. Satan just blinded them and their mind stopped.

The Shadow of God on Earth

It is difficult for a person to be lonely, or to live alone among a community that is against him and his beliefs. It is really a struggle, something that the Prophet ﷺ was praising. It is not easy. The Lord Almighty tested a *mureed* brother who was isolated, then so many people came and embraced Islam, giving *bay'ah* to Grandshaykh, and our brother was no longer alone. Plenty of people became interested in Islam, coming to Islam through the Naqshbandi Order.

A person may be interested in Buckingham Palace. If he is not going to see what is in it, such an interest means nothing. People now are interested in the Islamic sultanate, looking from outside and asking, "What is in it?" And so many people are cheated.

One of the first to be cheated is the Wahabis, who are telling people, "There is nothing in it. What you can see from the outside is Islam."

"But may we go inside?"

"There is no inside; it is only a building to look at from the outside. You must only look at it from the outside, there is nothing in it." That is their claim.

Such a huge building, the Islamic sultanate, and in its center is a throne. If there is a sultanate, there must be a throne, and if there is a throne, it cannot be without a sultan. Islam is not only international; it is the universal heavenly sultanate on earth. You must believe this. Satan is teaching people to be demagogues.

No one is saying, "O people, there must be a heavenly kingdom on earth, we must establish it." Why are they not saying this?

All believers in God, the Lord of heavens, the Lord Almighty—the Jews, Christians and Muslims—must come together, hand-in-hand, to ask the Lord to send the King of heavens to earth, to establish the Kingdom of heavens. But they are mindless people. If all of them would send their representatives to Jerusalem, Sham, Makkah, and Madinah, from morning to evening, in less than a day, Allah would send the heavenly king to earth. But they are only running after *dunya* (worldliness), asking to dress in shiny clothes and on their heads big crowns with jewels, carrying sticks and sitting on thrones, saying, "We are the kings of heavens on earth now."

But there is a divine chastisement coming to all nations, beginning with the religious people from all the faiths—religious "officials"—because all of them are claiming, "There is no need for someone from the heavens to be sultan of the divine sultanate on earth. We are enough—look at our dresses!"

They are too proud to accept anyone from the heavens, "No, we are living on earth, and we are not in need of heavenly people to come and be kings over us." Such proud "official" religious people represent different religions. Therefore, the first chastisement will be for them.

This must be well known: until the sultan appears on earth, difficulties and troubles among people will never end. In *Shari'ah* (divine law), the sultan is the shadow of the Lord on earth. You must ask, *Allāhumma, aj'al-lana min ladunka walīya, w 'aj'al-lana min ladunka sulṭānan naṣīra.*[42]

It is the teaching of the Holy Qur'an to ask the Lord Almighty for a sultan.

We hope that the sultan of the heavens will be on earth soon, will be with us, and collect people. The sultan of the heavens has the power, not only to gather the physical bodies, but he can gather the hearts of the people. The sultan of the heavens can collect the hearts. That is Sayyidina Mahdi ﷺ, and he is coming. All nations will come together through his heart, and he will be the king of the heavens for the divine kingdom on earth.

---

[42] "O Allah! From Your Presence grant us a protector and a supporting sultan (aiding our victory)."

May Allah bless you and make you to reach that heavenly sultan soon. *Ya Allah,* send us Your courageous nobles! This is an important message for all people: everything is in it. Fatiha.

Tie Your Camel

Bismillahi 'r-Rahmani 'r-Rahim—"in the name of God, the Compassionate, the Merciful." Last night something was stolen out of a car. How to deal with such cases? The *Shari'ah* is always answering for every event that humankind faces.

Once a Bedouin came to the Holy Prophet ﷺ on his camel. The Holy Prophet asked him, "What did you do with your camel?" The man replied, "I left it, and I am trusting in Allah that He is going to keep it safe." The Holy Prophet then said, "Go and tie your camel first, and then say, 'I am trusting in my Lord, the Lord Almighty.'"

First you, as a servant, must do what is your responsibility. Complete it and then, when you cannot do more than that, leave it to Allah. But not everything you may leave to Him. You may do some, and some is for Allah.

Grandshaykh told us:

> There was a *mureed* in Daghestan, who said, "I always leave my cattle outside at night, not bringing them into the stable, my house, because my shaykh is keeping them safe from the attack of wolves and violent animals." One day shaykh Abu Ahmad as-Sughuri, may Allah bless him and send his holy power on us, said to the *mureed*, "O, so-and-so Effendi, O my *mureed*, it is not good *adab* to make your shaykh a shepherd on the mountain all night. I am so weak, and it is so cold there."

This is an explanation for what the Prophet ﷺ was saying.

You did what was for you to do, and then, what shall we do? How did they open the car? He left the window a little bit open, and a satanic person lowered it, turning, and opening. In such a case, what is the Prophet saying? He is saying, "Make it *fee sabeelillah* (for the sake of Allah)."

Say, "I give for the sake of Allah what was stolen from me," and it's finished. The Holy Prophet said that for such people there is a special Paradise. It is only for them. But if someone is coming and asking to enter that Paradise, and what had been stolen from him, or what he had lost, was found later and he accepted it back, then it may be said to him, "Yes, you said *fee sabeelillah*, you gave it for the sake of Allah, but when it was found, you accepted it back. Now you cannot enter this Paradise."

One *Sahaba*, a son of the *khalif* Sayyidina 'Umar ♦, lost his beautiful, expensive red camel. He said, "*Fee sabeelillah* - for the sake of Allah," After some time, when he was sitting in the mosque, someone called, "O son of the *khalif*, your camel has just been found." He jumped up, but quickly sat down again, saying, *Astaghfirullah* – O God forgive me, because he remembered the *hadith* of The Holy Prophet ﷺ. He did it for the sake of Allah, and so he said, "It is for Allah, not for me now."

This is good manners, *adab*, that must be well known by everyone. So many things are going to be lost or stolen, and people get sad and cry. But this is what you should do; and you will find satisfaction through your heart by saying, "I did it for the sake of Allah. "

This is a holy month, Muharram, and some spiritually powerful people know that the money of some people is clean, earned honestly, through permitted means, *halal*, and they take that money and give it away for some purpose. They give it especially to the *Ahl al-Bayt*, people from the line of the Prophet. They are in very bad conditions in Bosnia, Kosova, Albania. It is not an ordinary person that knows and takes this money. Someone from the spiritually powerful people appeared to me, telling me this. Therefore, I am giving this *suhba* for the purpose that people around the whole world may benefit. The whole world and its treasures are not even as valuable as the wing of a fly. Do it for Allah, finished. He is giving more and more back to you. Now much more will come in this holy month to our brother, because everything in this month is one hundred times more than in other months. If you give *Fee sabeelillah* in this month, it must come back to you at least ten to one hundred times more.

May Allah keep us in His service, on His divine way. We, and everything we have, is for our Lord. Fatiha.

5. Hajj al-Akbar

Labbayk, Allahumma Labbayk: Here I am, O Lord, at Your Service

Pilgrims are preparing themselves today to climb up Mount Arafat, and tomorrow *insha-Allah* (God willing), they are going to be in the Divine Presence, standing up and asking the Lord Almighty to clean them of their sins, asking to be granted blessings from His endless mercy oceans.

Perhaps from the beginning until today there has never been such a crowded pilgrimage. Only this year it will happen, and it is important, because it is the last pilgrimage before the closing of the second millennium. Also, it is *Hajj al-Akbar* (the Great Pilgrimage) which, according to Islamic tradition, is honored seventy times more than an ordinary *Hajj* (pilgrimage).

Grandshaykh Abd Allah said that every year those who have been granted an invitation for *Hajj* come from every direction on earth. On the Day of Arafat (an integral rite of the pilgrimage), they are saying, *Labbayk, Allāhumma, labbayk*, which means:

O, our Lord, with our whole being, physical and spiritual, we are running to You, running after Your call, as You are calling us to come for *Hajj*, to visit Your holy house, the House of the Lord. We are running to You with all our humbleness. *Labbayk.* Just running to You. We are leaving everything and we are following Your call: *Labbayk Labbayk, Allāhumma, labbayk, labbayka lā sharīka laka, labbayk.* No one can be a partner to You. We have left everyone who is claiming to be Your partner. We are not hearing, not listening to them, we are not accepting their commands. We live only for You; we are running to You. We are weak servants, coming from the nation of Your true servant. *Labbayk, Allāhumma, labbayk, labbayka lā sharīka laka, labbayk, inna 'l-ḥamda, wa niʿamata, laka wa 'l-mulk, lā sharīka lak.*

Inna 'l-ḥamda. All glorifying, praising, absolute thanks that may be offered to You by Your servants; it is for You, only for You.

Wa niʿamata. What You are granting to us, Your servants, from every kind of *niʿamat* (favors and blessings), is from You only.

Laka wa 'l-mulk. Mulk, everything in existence including ourselves, belongs to You. *Lā sharīka laka.*

No one can say for even one spot, or one atom, or less than an atom, that it belongs to him. If anyone may say, "That atom belongs to me," Allah may tell him, "Take that smallest part that belongs to you, and go away!"

Or if anyone was saying, "That gigantic galaxy there is for me," the Lord may tell him, "Take it and go away, get out of My Territory!" To whoever may say this or that belongs to them, He may tell them to take it and go away. *Allahu Akbar, jalla jalaluhu.*

So tomorrow, when people are crowding on *Hajj*, calling to their Lord, the Veils of Greatness will open and the Lord Almighty will look at them, with a look that is just like one ray of the sun, or even less than that, coming and cleaning, cleaning, cleaning, until they are completely clean. This mercy is coming and covering people. Grandshaykh said that when it is *Hajj al-Akbar* (Grand *Hajj*, which occurs when the Day of Arafat is on a Friday), and the Lord Almighty is looking to His servants; that grant is coming to them seventy times, and therefore *Hajj al-Akbar* is equal to seventy pilgrimages.

Wahhabi people are not accepting this. They do not believe there is any *Hajj al-Akbar*. So we are taking the blessings and they are leaving them. Tomorrow is going to be that day, *insha-Allahu 'r-Rahman* (If God the Merciful Wills it).

There is one problem, or one point, that we may speak about. I have heard that the Wahhabi government and Wahhabi people are shaking now, because of the big crowds of pilgrims in Makkat al-Mukarrama. They are shaking, because they are counting over six million people now, but Allah knows; perhaps there are seven million or more. The Wahhabi School is a materialist current, never accepting any spirituality in Islam. They are materialist people, growing in Islam, who are thinking and writing about everything with their materialistic views, counting and balancing everything.

It was after the Second World War, 1946, and that year was also *Hajj al-Akbar*, the first time it occurred after the peace, and I was there with our Grandshaykh. Because of the war, not too many people could come, and everywhere was closed. I remember that more than two million pilgrims were there, and at that time there were still the old buildings in Makkat al-Mukarrama and Madinat al-Munawwarah that the Ottomans had built.

I remember that when we prayed our last Juma prayer in the *Haram* of Makka, *sharafaha Allah,* may Allah honor it more, at least one million people, maybe more, were praying there, and according to the size of the area of the *Haram ash-Sharif*, only one hundred and fifty thousand people could enter it, no more. I prayed inside the *Haram*, and yet around the Ka'aba there were empty places for some people. I was there.

Wahabis are saying that they must help the people, and in this they are really claiming that they must help Allah. *Astaghfirullah*, making an extension of Makkat al-Mukarrama for people to take their rest in, to enter it freely, to do *tawaf* freely, to pray freely, with no crowding of people. They began renovations. But as much as they were making extensions, bigger crowds were coming.

I went year after year—1980 was the last *Hajj* for me that my physical being was there also—and I could never reach to do the Juma prayer inside those buildings. Always I was outside, praying with others out on the street.

And now that they have made it so big they are realizing, "O, we have destroyed Makkah, but people are still not able to pray comfortably in the *Haram*." They also destroyed Madinat al-Munawwarah, yet it is not big enough for people.

So Satan was teaching them, saying, "Make contingents, limits." That means they are now doing something else that is not *Rahmani*, but *Shaytani,* because it is Satan who teaches them to make limits in who or how many pilgrims may enter the holy sites.

They made so many tunnels under the mountains in Saudi, ways to reach Mina and then Arafat. The more they are trying to do something, the more they are becoming *majnun* (crazy), all of them. It would be so simple: do not touch anything! It is an invitation from the Lord Almighty to the people. Whomever He is asking to come and visit His holy house, He is carrying responsibility for His visitors, not human beings!

The Wahhabis are like rocks; their heads are like rocks, never understanding anything about spirituality. That is the reason why they are shaking now, asking, "What shall we do?" Leave people free! Makkah and Madinah are for all the Muslims; why put such foolish limits on people? Leave them to come and visit. If they were leaving the matter to Allah, even sixty million people could come easily, because angels would put roads under them, ways to move, to come and go smoothly.

I have heard that they have also destroyed everything inside the *Haram ash-Sharif* (the Divine Sanctuary of Makkah) to make *tawaf* (circumambulation of the Ka'aba) easy, but that now people make *tawaf* outside, in big circles. What is that?

I was there in 1946, and at both ends of Safa and Marwa (the two holy hills included in the rites of *Hajj*) there were shops, and also camels passing on the way and cars and people going like this, coming like that, crossing the way. We, the pilgrims, were performing *sa'i* (a rite of *Hajj* where pilgrims trot between the hills Safa and Marwa) and passing so easily, with more than two million people. Now, if they are able to, they are going to make seven floors for people, but even if they make seventy floors, people will not be able to make their *sa'i* as freely as we were making it.

Sometimes we were running into the camels, because they were getting up on the way, and it was at that place that we had to run. And we were running and there were cars with donkeys passing, and we could not continue. But we were so happy, making *sa'i*. Now, *subhanallah*. Take your hands from the Holy House, al-Haram ash-Sharif! Leave it to Allah, and Madinat al-Munawwarah to Prophet Muhammad ﷺ!

The Wahhabi officials are shaking now. "How can we control the situation?" Leave it; there is another controller there, *Muhafiz-u-Mecca* (Protector of Makkah, i.e., God). It is not an ordinary place. They think it is an ordinary place, because there is no spirituality with them. Everything they are counting, making an account.

Tomorrow, *insha-Allah*, should be that biggest *Hajj* which closes this century, and another opening is coming, *insha-Allah*. We have been informed that Sahib-uz-Zaman, Sayyidina Mahdi ؏, and his *khulafa* and 12,000 *awliya*, who all have the power to reach there in a blink of an eye, should be there tomorrow. And it should be a strong *munajat*, *du'a*, prayer, which will change everything this year, *insha-Allah*, we hope.

It is a special *Hajj*. For whoever is prevented from reaching it this year and they had prepared themselves but the government told them, "No way for you," the Lord Almighty is sending angels on their behalf. Also for common people who said, "If only we could reach Arafat," and they were not able to, Allah has created angels to be on Arafat on their behalf, to reach those favors from Him.

Tomorrow you must try to complete:

- 1000 *Sūratu 'l-Ikhlāṣu 'sh-Sharīf*

- 1000 *lā ilāha ill-Allāh*
- 1000 ṣalawāt: *Allāhumma ṣalli ʿalā Muḥammadin wa ʿalā āli Muḥammadin wa sallim*
- 100 *Lā ilāhā ill-Allāh, wāḥdahū lā sharīka lah, lahu 'l-mulku wa lahu 'l-ḥamd, yuḥī wa yūmīt, wa Hūwa ʿalā kulli shay'in qadīr*
- 100 *wa lā ḥawla wa lā quwwata illa billāhi 'l-ʿAlīyyi 'l-ʿĀẓīm*
- And at every prayer to make the *takbīr: Allāhu Akbar, Allāhu Akbar, lā ilāha ill-Allāh, w 'Allāhu Akbar, Allāhu Akbar wa li'llāhi'l ḥamd.*[43]

May Allah send His divine servants to take away everything that is against Him. May He send His lions on jackals, wolves, foxes, bears, snakes and scorpions[44], to take them away.

I am asking, "O our Lord, no doubt You have lions, and even one is enough. You send angels to Your most beloved servant Muhammad ﷺ on the days of Uhud and Badr[45], and even one angel was enough to take away the whole army of hypocrites; but You sent thousands of them, so that the believers were looking and seeing angels among them and they got the certainty that they would be victorious. Therefore, even one lion is enough, we know, more than enough, but we are asking for Your lions to come and remove the sultanate of Satan and take away the satanic kingdom on earth!"

If He is asking to put one billion people in this place here, He can do it, and everyone may come and go freely. One billion people may be in this small place. He can do it; you must believe in Allah, must believe in His endless power and ability, His capacity. There are endless possibilities for Him only, the Almighty. Why are you trying to do something? As much as you are doing these wrong actions, more difficulties are coming, more troubles, and crises.

It was so easy the first and second times on *Hajj*, until they began to destroy everything: old houses, at that time there were no concrete buildings

---

[43] Refer to Chapter 14 for translation.

[44] metaphors for bad human characteristics

[45] Crucial battles in which the first generation of Muslims defended their faith against the idolaters who aggressively sought to eliminate the Prophet and his followers.

at all, and they destroyed every historic building, all of them. They made huge concrete buildings, so that people are no longer able to breathe spirituality in Makkat al-Mukarramah and Madinat al-Munawwarah. People's feelings have become confused, and they are saying, "Where are we?"

Insha-Allah, when Mahdi ﷺ comes, he will set right what was wronged. That is *irada,* willpower. When someone is given that willpower, he may say, "Be (*kun fa yakoon*)" and it will occur. The Lord Almighty is saying, "O My servant, be obedient to Me, and I will make you of My staff *(rabbani),* and I will give you the power and authority to say for something: 'Be' and it will be."

Therefore, if Imam Mahdi ﷺ orders those buildings to be taken away, in one night they will be finished, and the second night, when he is ordering to be brought back the same buildings as were destroyed before in Makkat al-Mukarramah and Madinat al-Munawwarah, it will be as it was. People will run smoothly, make *tawaf* smoothly, and move smoothly to Mina and Arafat[46], *insha-Allah.* Fatiha.

O My Servant, Come Visit Me

May Allah bless the *Ummat-ul-habib*, the nation of Prophet Muhammad ﷺ, the most honored nation. We are proud, and we are thanking the Lord Almighty for granting us to be from the nation of His most honored, most glorified and praised Servant, Prophet Muhammad ﷺ.

Tonight is the fourth night of the *Eid* in Makkat al-Mukarramah, and people are running around the house of the Lord, making *tawaf.* We have been called and invited, ordered and offered to make a visit to His glorified and praised Holy House. It is an Honored House, and the glory of this building does not come from its outward appearance, no. It is a very simple building; there is nothing special about its design or architecture. It is so simple, it only has four walls.

There is a good saying, that in reality, the honor of a place is according to who is there—*sharafu 'l-maqām fi 'l-muqīm*—and not with its buildings and its qualities. Honor and glory are given to that place according to who is

[46] Integral rituals of the Hajj.

in it. Therefore, for the reason that the Seal of Prophets was in Madinat al-Munawwarah and is buried there, that city is honored and glorified. Allah gives so much honor and lights to it. And in Makkat al-Mukarramah, for that simple building to be the house of the Lord gives it honor and glory. Without that quality, that place could not give anything. But when they say, 'house of the Lord', people ask to come. We have been ordered and invited to visit that holy house, because it is the House of the Lord (*Baytullah*). If it was an empty place, no one would ask to visit it. If there were no one in this *dargah*, if the shaykh was not there, people would say, "Why are we going to Lefke? We have so many *dargahs*, so many buildings, we may go there. We only come to visit Lefke and the *dargah* for the honor of the shaykh."

People have been offered to visit the House of the Lord, and they are running, not to visit the house, but the Lord of the house. That is the House of the Lord, but people are asking for the Lord of that house, that is the difference.

Hajj is one of the most important pillars of Islam. The five pillars of Islam begin with *Iman*, the belief in your Lord the Lord Almighty and the Testimony of Faith, the Shahada: *Lā ilāha illa-Allāh Muḥammadun Rasūl Allāh*. The other pillars are five times prayer, fasting in the holy month of *Ramadan*, *zakat*, and the *Hajj*[47], so that the principles of our belief begin with the faith in the Lord, and end by visiting Him. For believers in the Lord of the House, the House of the Lord is waiting for their visit, that they may visit Him.

Finally, you who say, "I believe in the Lord the Lord Almighty, *amantu billahi,*" must run to visit your Lord, because finally the Lord Almighty is asking for His servant, "O My servant, come and visit Me at My house of the Lord; you must come and visit Me."

If you are prepared, a way is going to be open for you to meet the Lord of the House. You may hear, you may see, you may feel, and you may be with Him. Grandshaykh said that a genuine *hajji* is the one who goes and says, "*As-salamu 'alaykum, ya Baytullah,*" and hears the reply, "*Wa 'alaykum salam, ya 'Abdi,* O My servant." This is for special servants. For others, "*Wa 'alaykum salam, ya Abd Allah.*" If he is a prepared one, an answer is coming, and he is hearing.

---

[47] Refer to the glossary for definitions.

It is very important; you are reaching that rank step-by-step, *alhamdulillah*. Whoever is working for Allah is never tiring. Our physical body is getting tired, but there is a state when even the physical body is not tiring anymore. *We* are asking to reach to that point.

No doubt, Allah is the Absolute Sultan, from pre-eternity up to eternity, and the Absolute Sultanate is for Him only. May the sultan of *Shari'ah* (divine law) come soon with Allah's blessings, and may we be with him forever on *Shari'atullah* (God's Law). Fatiha.

Keep Allah and Allah Will Keep You

[A number of *mureeds* visit the Shaykh after having gone for the pilgrimage].

It was *Hajj al-Akbar* in 1999, the last *Hajj al-Akbar* of the twentieth century and the second millennium. You are lucky people that you have been there. The next *Hajj al-Akbar* is going to be in the third millennium, the 21st century according to the Christian calendar. According to the Islamic calendar, Sayyidina Mahdi ؑ is going to be with us in a *Hajj al-Akbar*.

You were lucky that this year Mahdi ؑ and his caliphs and ministers, all these grand *awliya* (saints), were present on the day of Arafat (an integral ritual of hajj, the annual pilgrimage to Makkah). All 12,000 of them were with Sayyidina Mahdi ؑ. He made his last prayers when the sun was setting on Friday evening. From the Lord Almighty the good tidings came through His most respected and beloved servant, Prophet Muhammad ﷺ, that all their prayers were accepted. On Friday evening, the beginning of Saturday, when you moved to Mina after sunset, Divine Orders changed to bring faith up and to put unbelief down.

It is becoming impossible now for the unbelievers. Their hegemony is going to finish, and the sultanate of Satan is going to be taken away. *Haqq*, the Truth that Allah sent, will appear now day by day, and hour by hour it will increase. Truth will conquer falsehood, and the believers will overpower the unbelievers.

May Allah bless you and your Hajj, your charities, and visits to holy places. You have been in Sham and visited everywhere, and Grandshaykh accepted you and gives his *salams,* greetings of peace, to all of you. He was happy and proud of you, because you came by his way to the Holy Prophet ﷺ, and the Prophet was happy with you too, looking to you and blessing you.

Now you are on your way home, and there is going to be a new opening for you and around you. Those Divine Lights granted to you through Grandshaykh from the Holy Prophet ﷺ are going to spread, and people should run from their darkness to your light.

Who keeps his heart with Allah, Allah will be with him. If you are not leaving Allah, He is not going to leave you. Therefore, as The Holy Prophet was saying, "Keep Allah and Allah will keep you."[48] There are going to be many good tidings for you, for every true one, and trustworthy people are going to be happy in this year.

We are happy and proud of you. You came such a long distance to visit the Prophet ﷺ and the house of the Lord. You are young people, not easily going to be tired, but it is not an ordinary trip. It is a journey of obedience and worship, and worship is always going to be difficult for our ego. Every time we carry difficulties, we are paid more blessings by the Lord Almighty.

Also, Mahdi ؏ pointed out our group of pilgrims from western countries. He said, "Look, Shaykh Abd Allah's *mureed*s, Naqshbandi followers," and he was so happy, looking to that group who went there keeping the Sunnah, and giving them some spirituality that was never given to other people. *Alhamdulillah*, they were very happy with you. May Allah bless you.

Some brothers from Chile came to me in London during Ramadan. They have built a new mosque in the south of Chile, the most southern place on earth near the South Pole. *Alhamdulillah*, there is now much more spirituality running through the hearts of people, because they are in need of spirituality more than anything else.

Bi hurmati'l-habib, bi hurmati'l-sirri Surat al-Fatiha.

About Sayyidina Imam Mahdi

Bismillahi 'r-Rahmani 'r-Rahim—"*in the name of God, the Compassionate, the Merciful.*" Sayyidina Mahdi's ؏ first appearance was in Hijaz, in Makkah on Mount Arafat. It was a private appearance, only for saints. Twelve thousand

---

[48] Tirmidhi, Abd ibn Humaid and *Musnad* Ahmad.

awliya came and put their hands on his hand, taking *bay'ah* (allegiance) with him.

Once, when I was passing through Beirut on my way to Cyprus, I met a shaykh from Lebanon and was a guest in his house. He asked me, "What news is your shaykh giving about Mahdi ﷺ?"

I told him, that many years ago we were on Arafat with Mahdi ﷺ and 12,000 *rijalu'llah, awliya,* and that we all took *bay'ah* with Mahdi ﷺ, and I was with Grandshaykh at that time. He took me with him, like a hunter keeps his dog with him.

The shaykh from Lebanon answered, "You are right. I was in Makkat al-Mukarrama the same year with my shaykh, and we met a person from the Sudan."

We asked him, "From where are you coming?" He told us that he had come from Central Africa.

He said, "One year ago I was ordered by the Holy Prophet ﷺ to be here this year to take *bay'ah* with Mahdi ﷺ and I have been walking on foot for one year, and reached here."

The *awliya* have already taken *bay'ah* with Mahdi ﷺ in that year. There is a second kind of *bay'ah*, in dreams, for people who are not prepared to meet Mahdi ﷺ physically. Now he is waiting for the order, and then common people will take *bay'ah* with him.

He will appear for all people, according to the Lord's command, in the Great War (Armageddon). There are 101 hindrances that he must overcome, before he can appear.[49] Ninety-nine of those hindrances have passed. Now only two remain.

'Red-colored people'[50] have come to Afghanistan. They must also come to Pakistan, and then to Turkey. That is the first sign: 'Red ones' coming to Turkey. Huge 'red' powers will be concentrated west of Aleppo. They will come up to the plain of Yarmuq. At the same time western powers will be in Adana, near the sea. There will be a great battle in that plain. The war will last three months, during which Mahdi ﷺ will appear. It will be in a year of the Hajj al-Akbar.

---

[49] i.e. events predicted to take place before his appearance.

[50] i.e. communists.

Mahdi ﷺ will appear on Hajj, where people will take *bay'ah* with him. From there he will go to Sham. He will make *takbir* three times: *Allahu Akbar, Allahu Akbar, Allahu Akbar*! With those *takbirs* the harmful problem of technology is going to be finished.

There are forty stations on Sayyidina Mahdi's way between Makkah and Sham. He will come to the gates of Sham, first to a place where the footprints of the Prophet Muhammad ﷺ and his camel are on a stone. He will enter Sham, and there the people will take initiation, *bay'ah*, with him.

Then there are seven stations on his way from Sham to Istanbul—Homs, Hama, Trablus, Halep, Konya, Bursa—and in Istanbul he will take out the flag of the Prophet ﷺ from Topkapi Palace. But before that, the Padishah will appear and they will meet in Konya, where Mahdi ﷺ will take up the *amanat* (trusts) of the Prophet ﷺ including his *jubbah* (cloak).

After Mahdi has taken out the flag in Istanbul, the Anti-Christ will come quickly through Khorasan and run to Quds, to go around the whole world from there for forty days. He is now in chains—imprisoned on an unknown island that no one can approach—because he is saying, "I am your Lord," claiming to be the Lord of humankind, not just a prophet, but the Lord! He cannot move from there. He is Satan, the father of all devils. He is giving orders, and he has thirty deputies who are preparing people for his coming. He is one-eyed.

Jews are expecting the Messiah. Christians are expecting Jesus Christ to come back from the heavens, too. Muslims are expecting Sayyidina Mahdi ﷺ and also Sayyidina 'Isa ﷺ (Jesus Christ) to come from the heavens. All people of faith are expecting a global change for this earth.

There will be a heavenly announcement, "The enemy of Allah, Dajjal, has appeared. Whoever wants to save himself must go to Sham, Makkah or Madinah."

So believers will run because Dajjal (the anti-Christ) will be after them. They will run like streams to Sham, and all believers must be there for forty days. Dajjal will go around the whole world, but 700 angels, 700 jinn, and 700 *awliya* from Budala, Nujaba, Nuqaba, Awtad and Akhyar will protect Sham, so he will not be able to enter.

Sham is a holy area, the place where the Judgment Day would eventually take place. There, twice a day, comes *Nur*, Divine Lights, and Mercy. This area covers all that a man can see from the minaret of the

Umayyad Mosque, and its *baraka,* blessings, spread for a distance of six or seven days camel ride in all directions.

After forty days, Jesus will come down from the heavens. It will be the time of the *Fajr* prayer, when he comes down in the Umayyad Mosque in Sham. He is coming down to a minaret of that dome in the east, under which Sayyidina Yahya ﷺ (John the Baptist) is buried. Two angels will protect him with their wings, and bring him down to earth.

He will be wearing a green turban, and he will be shining. He has the most beautiful face, rosy and white. His beard is red, he is sweating, and he has a sword. When he was on earth, he never touched a sword, but now he is coming as a savior, to save people from the hands of the Anti-Christ. His sword is a miraculous sword, a heavenly sword of light. It can reach any point to where he sends it. The Lord gave it to him.

He is not coming as a prophet anymore, but as a member of the nation of Prophet Muhammad ﷺ, following his *Shari'ah.* Sayyidina Mahdi ﷺ will offer the place to Jesus ﷺ to be *imam,* but Jesus ﷺ will refuse. Sayyidina Mahdi ﷺ will lead the prayer once, and after that Jesus ﷺ will be *imam.* Sayyidina Mahdi ﷺ will be with him for seven years.

Jesus ﷺ will defeat the Anti-Christ, and make clear the truth about himself and his mother, Sayyida Maryam ﷺ. He will govern the heavenly kingdom on earth for forty years. In his time, all technology will be taken away, and in its place everyone will be given miraculous powers, so that when you look somewhere and you say, *Bismillahi 'r-Rahmani 'r-Rahim —"in the name of God, the Compassionate, the Merciful.* By Your Divine permission, O My Lord! You honored me to be Your deputy. I ask of You," and if He gives permission, you may put your step from here to there.

After Jesus ﷺ has defeated the Anti-Christ, there will be no more evil in his time. People will live as if they are in Paradise, and Paradise appearances (*tajalliyat*) will come on them. At that time, the purpose of Allah's creation will appear. Sayyidina Isa ﷺ will marry and have children. When he is going to die, he will be buried in Madinah, in the fourth tomb next to the Holy Prophet ﷺ, Sayyidina Abu Bakr ﷺ, and Sayyidina 'Umar ﷺ, which is empty now.

Then all believers will die by a sweet scent from Paradise. Everything terrible after that will come to the unbelievers, who will have started to reappear during Jesus' time. Then the world will come to its end.

God's Deputy

Muhammad al-Mahdi ﷺ is a descendant of the Holy Prophet Muhammad ﷺ, through his daughter Fatimah az-Zahra ﷺ and her sons, Sayyidina Hasan ﷺ and Sayyidina Husayn ﷺ in the fortieth generation. So he is a Sayyid, Hasani and Husayni. His parents live near Jeddah.

He was born between in the Wadi Fatimah, a green valley on the way from Jeddah to Madinah. When he was growing up, miraculous looks started to come out of him. He had such lights. The gazes of people started to come very much on him because his growth was miraculous. He has a spot of ashes on his right cheek, like a star, and his arms reach to his knees.

By the order of the Prophet ﷺ, he was taken away from people by the *awliya*—Nuqaba, Nujaba, Budala, Awtad and Akhyar, whose *imam* is Shahabu'ddin—to a place behind the Mountain of Qaf. Then he was ordered to remain in the Empty Quarter, the Rub' al-Khali, a desert between Saudi Arabia and Yemen. No one can go there, because there is quicksand, moving sands. He is not living with ordinary people now, because he has such heavy power that people cannot look at him.

He is living in that desert with his 99 caliphs, highly spiritual, powerful people. There is a huge cave; its entrance is forty meters wide. In that cave is the 'Dome of Happiness', which has been built by the angels. No one can approach that cave because it is protected by jinns, who send out electricity that keeps them away. Mahdi ﷺ and his caliphs are there, waiting for and expecting the holy command of the Lord Almighty to appear. Sayyidina Mahdi ﷺ is the most spiritual person on earth now, and all *awliya* are under his command.

When he appears, he will say, "*Allahu Akbar, Allahu Akbar, Allahu Akbar*—God is Great!" three times, in Sham, and this will be heard from East to West.

The archangel Gabriel ﷺ will shout, "*Khalifatullah* (the Lord Almighty's deputy) has just appeared! Join his group, O believers!"

Everything will be clear. Sayyidina Mahdi ﷺ will appear with such a spiritual power that all technology will stop. Sayyidina Mahdi ﷺ is coming as a savior before Sayyidina 'Isa ﷺ to save people in that time of tribulation.

All the technology is under the control of jinns, so nothing will be by chance. Everything is just arranged. There is a group of saints, the five pole saints, *qutbs*, who look after everything according to the Will of Allah. Nothing on this earth happens by chance or accident, or without a reason.

The followers of the Anti-Christ, are those who are running after this life's pleasures, following materialistic thoughts, seeking pleasures that their egos are asking for, asking for every freedom. There are people who always come into contact with the devil, falling under his control, and supporting the kingdom of Satan. They will be with the Anti-Christ because they are evil in themselves. The devils will carry them to the source of evil and devils, the Anti-Christ.

Many of humankind are now following satanic teachings, supporting the kingdom of devils on earth, and that is why a storm will come as a chastisement, blowing from East to West, North to South. The supporters of the saviors, Sayyidina Mahdi ﷺ and Jesus Christ ﷺ will be saved.

At that time divine shelter will be for those who do not harm others, and obedient faithful people who avoid prohibited or harmful things to others or to themselves. Therefore, everybody must try to prevent his ego from doing bad things and from having bad intentions. If not, there will be no shelter; nothing and no one can protect them. Therefore, to believe is the first shelter. Another important shelter is to believe in the right way.

For some people their good character will be a shelter; people with good intentions, who are compassionate, helpful, just and respectful towards others, loving them. Another shelter is to give charity and to pray and make *sajda* (prostration in worship), the Lord Almighty is promising to shelter good servants. Therefore everybody must ask how he can be a good one.

Now everything is mixed up; truth with untruth, goodness with badness, purity with dirtiness. Until the last events come, the times will get worse and worse. When Jesus Christ ﷺ comes he will put everything in its proper place, and no one will object. The 21st century will be the century of truth and reality.

In the Last Days, so many men will pass on. There will be many more women than men. This is because men are mostly cruel. From seven people, one will remain. For those women who do not have a husband anymore, Allah will send people from behind the Mountain of Qaf, so that no one will be alone in that time. When Sayyidina Mahdi ﷺ comes, he will bring with him so many people from unknown worlds around this earth: Nuqaba, Nujaba, Budala, Awtad and Akhyar.

After that time of difficulty, everywhere will be open for the peace-loving faithful people who harmed no one. According to their *kismet*, destiny, which is written on the Lawh-ul-Mahfoudh (the Preserved Tablet), Sayyidina Mahdi ☆ will show everyone their place.

After this people's hearts will be like seeds ready for planting. Sayyidina Mahdi ☆ will open the seed of faith in their hearts, opening the hearts of the believers who lived through that difficulty. Common people will be dressed sainthood and will be granted miraculous powers and lights from the Lord Almighty. *Awliya* will be love-springs. People will be perfect servants of Allah, living on prayer and *dhikr*, and swimming in love oceans. Everywhere you will find the love of the Lord. Creatures will take from you that Divine Love. We are created for that. The perfection of creation should appear in those days.

No one will be interested in eating or drinking, and if they should ask to eat something, light quality natural food should come from the skies. Everyone will take his share and *dhikr* should burn it, so there will be no need for toilets. May Allah make us reach those days. *Bi hurmati'l-habib.* Fatiha.

Not Only a Hope, but Reality

We have been ordered to say something about these miraculous times and events that are approaching soon, to make your unhappiness change to happiness, and to make you more patient. As much as you can hear and believe, you can reach happiness quickly. It is not only a hope, it is going to be a reality for you to be able to see Jesus Christ and Mahdi ☆.

A person may be sentenced to forty years of prison and be told that after these forty years he will be set free with someone's help, and be king of the country. Will his sufferings affect him? Forty years of prison is suffering, but he knows that his suffering will end and that a kingdom will come to him. Joseph, Sayyidina Yusuf ☆, was a Prophet, and he was imprisoned, but it did not affect him because he was told through his dream that he would be the King of Egypt.

Suffering is only for those who have no hope of a second life, of an eternal life. We know that the whole world is full of suffering, but that hope, our faith, our beliefs, can take all of that away from us. But those who do not believe will always come under heavy burdens. So we are trying to give to everyone hope for an eternal life, so that they can carry everything with enjoyment, and not be overcome with all their suffering. That is important. You cannot know now, you cannot see it now. Therefore, you must believe, because you cannot know until you are in it. Belief is something, but knowledge is something else. May Allah grant us strong belief. Fatiha.

6. Healing and Purification of Hearts

Prophet Muhammad: The Healer of Hearts

The Holy Prophet ﷺ said, "In the body of Man there is a piece of flesh. If it is healthy, the whole body is healthy. This piece of flesh is the heart."[51]

The heart is most important, as it is the seat of Man's reality, of his personality and character. The heart's health depends on faith.

Health comes through sincerity, illness through hypocrisy. Health comes through love of Allah, illness through love of *dunya*. Health comes through contentedness, illness through greed. Health comes through gentleness, illness though anger. Health comes through the remembrance of the Lord, *dhikr*, illness through heedlessness, forgetting Allah. Health means being with Allah, illness means to forget Allah and to be with Satan.

There are so many spiritual illnesses of the heart: hypocrisy, polytheism, showing off, pride, greed, envy, jealousy, hatred, stubbornness, love of this world, egoism, lying, backbiting, bad intentions. Whoever has any of these characteristics is ill and in need of treatment.

The Prophet came to cure hearts. There was no illness, physical or spiritual, which he could not heal. He cured his Companions, the *Sahaba*, and raised them in rank, so that they became like stars in the sky. Then the Companions became doctors themselves and cured others. Those who followed them, the *Tabi'een*, became healers, too, and so on until today.

Every saint, inheritor of the Prophet, has the ability to give medicine to people for physical and spiritual illnesses. If anyone wants to know about the condition of his heart, he must go to someone who knows. But nowadays, people are so proud that they think they can cure themselves. They accept neither saints, nor scholars, nor other people of knowledge. But even a chief doctor calls another doctor for help when he is ill. He does not stand in front of a mirror and cure himself. It is a Divine command to

---

[51] *Sahih Bukhari.*

consult those who are always in the Divine Presence, because the answers that come to their heart are sent to them by Allah Himself.

The Real Doctors

Who is a genuine doctor? He is the one saving people from bad characteristics, giving them good attributes. Ordinary physicians save people from temporary death, but a bad character may cause eternal death. As much as people are not interested in eternal life, so many troubles are raining on them. As much as they are interested in eternal life, troubles are going away.

It is important for a physician to have inspiration to make a diagnosis. As much as a physician has a pure heart, he easily understands sickness, and prescribes a medicine. This is possible if he is beyond the love of money, only thinking of helping people and lightening suffering. Then Allah takes the veil from his heart and then he is successful. By helping people, Allah will help you. Most lovely to Allah is someone helping others. It is an honor for everyone. We must intend everyday to help others, not to help ourselves, and then Allah will help us. His help is enough. If every person on earth gathered to help you, they could not do what He can. He gives pleasure, safety and satisfaction. You cannot buy it. This is only for sincere servants.

You must ask for power from the Lord Almighty's power oceans so that you can be able to help His servants.

Signs of a Spiritual Guide

The sign of a *murshid* (shaykh, spiritual guide) is that you are able to trust him. Your heart gives the signal and the heart is never mistaken. If a person is sitting with a true murshid, he feels peace, rest and satisfaction, very happy. This is the sign. He forgets all of his troubles in his presence and feels just like a fish in the ocean. Why do people go to the seaside? Because when they enter the water, they find rest and enjoyment. The soul is also asking for an ocean. In our lives we need one person who is like an ocean, so that our hearts can enjoy and be satisfied with that person.

We have such bad characteristics. We need someone to give us good attributes; and they do not come through reading books but through one's friends. By looking at a person's friends, you may know his character. A bad character is contagious, like a sickness. Therefore, the Lord Almighty sent prophets as medicine. Prophets are not angels; they are of humankind, and know everything about human nature. Whoever sits with them absorbs good characteristics.

As You Like, O My Lord!

As much as you believe in your shaykh, you may give the reins over to his hands, and so find rest and satisfaction in your heart. As long as you are trying to catch the reins in your own hands, you are carrying a great burden on your shoulders.

Shaykhs are the inheritors of the prophets who are offering to carry your burdens, and you must give your burdens to them. Just put your desires in line with the shaykh's; that is the way to open your heart to heavenly power. Then you may see, or hear, or know something that you cannot know now.

So many *mureeds* have high spiritual aspiration, *himma*, and they say, "O my shaykh, I am asking for *himma* in order that my soul may be activated."

The shaykh replies, "O my disciple, I am asking service from you, *khidma*. You must be like me. When you are like me, my spiritual powers may come to you; but if we are not of the same kind of metal, the current cannot pass through you. I am copper, and you must not remain stone."

The Lord Almighty asked the Prophet ﷺ to be with Him, and the Prophet asked the Companions to be with him. To be 'with him' meant for them to be as he wished them to be. The shaykh also asks *mureeds* to be 'with him.'

The Prophet ﷺ said of Abu Bakr ؓ that he had "died before he died," because he had absolutely left all his desires behind, so that there was nothing left of them in the face of his Lord and his Prophet. Abu Bakr ؓ lost all desire for this life. When he arrived at this state, he was like a shadow of the Prophet ﷺ, entirely in agreement with him, never leaving his way. Because of this attribute, Abu Bakr ؓ became trustworthy in all respects, and thus the Prophet ﷺ was able to plant many types of knowledge in his heart. Therefore, in spiritual rank, Abu Bakr was at the top of all companions of the Prophet ﷺ.

The Prophet ﷺ praised him, saying that if his faith was balanced against the faith of the whole Ummah, Abu Bakr's faith would be heavier.

On the Day of Promises, when everyone was asked by the Lord Almighty, "Am I not your Lord?" and we replied, "Yes, You are our Lord," on that day, if it had not been for Abu Bakr teaching everyone with his spiritual power, no one could have said, "Yes."

Our Grandshaykh said that everyone has a share of Abu Bakr's faith, even the person of the lowest degree of faith. From that share, whether they pray or not, so many people will go to Paradise, because it keeps people from a bad ending in this life and the next. *Lā ilāha illa-Allāh Muḥammadun Rasūl Allāh* ﷺ is written in the heart; it only needs a chance to show itself.

So many people have the seeds of faith in their hearts, deeply planted, only waiting for mercy rain. Mercy may be delayed up to the end; a person may be on his deathbed and begin to cry. This crying attracts that mercy, the Lord Almighty says, "My servant is crying," and the seed of faith opens, filling the heart, green with the lights of genuine faith. He was like a desert, then death comes, and he begins to cry. That is the sign of mercy coming on him. Allah does not leave His servants; He has endless mercy.

The Prophet ﷺ said about Abu Bakr, "Whatever Allah has put in my heart I have poured into the heart of Abu Bakr."[52]

Sayyidina 'Ali ؓ also put his will and desires totally in line with the Prophet's desires. Therefore, the Prophet ﷺ said about him, "I am the City of Knowledge, and Ali is its gate."[53]

There are forty-one *tariqats* to make our hearts pure: forty spring from the heart of Imam Ali, and one, the Naqshbandi Order, is coming from Abu Bakr as-Siddiq ؓ. The Prophet ﷺ had 124,000 companions, and Abu Bakr was the highest companion. This is well known among genuine *tariqah* shaykhs who do not give titles to themselves. They respect the Naqshbandi Order as the first one.

A genuine shaykh must know if a disciple was with him on the Day of Promises or not. He has light in his eyes and recognizes his *mureed*s without

---

52 Shaykh Muhammad Sulayman, *al-Hadiqa an-Nadiyya.*

53 Narrated by al-Hakim and rigorously authenticated (*sahih*), also from at-Tirmidhi with chains from Jabir and Ali; at-Tirmidhi and as-Suyuti declared it to be good (*hasan*)

mistake. You may meet many shaykhs and take exercises, but not find satisfaction until finding your Grandshaykh. So many shaykhs are only trainers, but a Grandshaykh must finally call you. This does not happen through words; but there are ways from heart to heart. If a Naqshbandi shaykh is giving *bay'ah*, he must tell the disciple who the Grandshaykh is in his time for the Naqshbandi Order. He must point to him.

So many people from the West are coming now, invited by the way of hearts to our Grandshaykh. The Golden Chain of Grandshaykhs ends in our Grandshaykh, the last link in the chain. I am only his servant. We are waiting for the Naqshbandi shaykhs to come and renew their *bay'ah* with us. If not, they are just putting titles on themselves. There may be a thousand shaykhs, but only one Grandshaykh. If they come together, who will be the Imam? If all of the 124,000 Sahaba are brought together, who is the Imam? Sayyidina Abu Bakr.

Sayyidina Mahdi ﷺ and his seven grand *wazirs*, 99 *khalifahs*, and 313 grand *murshids* are all in the Naqshbandi *tariqah*. In these times, there is no power for other *tariqats* to carry people all the way to the ultimate goal. All are invited to renew their *bay'ah* with our Grandshaykh, and they may observe their improvement.

Both Abu Bakr and Ali reached their divine positions and took their holy trusts from the Prophet ﷺ during their lifetime. Because they desired and did what the Prophet ﷺ desired and did, they reached a station where they were shown Prophet Muhammad's ﷺ real prophetic personality in the Divine Presence.

If we can use our willpower as we should, making it accord with our Lord's desires, carrying out our Lord's Will, then we may improve to reach the ranks of saints and prophets, approach the Divine Presence and be accepted there. The Lord Almighty has said, through all of His holy prophets, "O My people, if you claim that you are servants, then put your desires in line with Mine, otherwise you are not servants. I am not in need of your worship; all I want from you is that you accord with My Desires."

We have to learn manners and keep a form of discipline, so we can say inside ourselves, "As You like, O My Lord."

Maqam al-Ihsan: The Station of Sincerity

We must be sincere believers. As servants, we must know that the Lord Almighty is watching us all the time, and that He is with us, wherever we are: *Huwa ma'akum ayna ma kuntum.*[54] We are living through Him; how can anyone or anything exist without Him? Therefore, He is always with us, reaching us everywhere, like the government. If you know there is a hidden camera, do not you drive slowly? This is the meaning of the *Ihsan Maqam*, the Station of Sincerity, leaving imitated faith and reaching to true belief. We have to direct ourselves towards Allah, always fulfilling His Rights first, then to look after *dunya*, worldly things.

Our Conscience Is from Heavens

We must choose our Lord's pleasure. If we listen to our conscience, we can know goodness from badness, permissible (*halal*) from forbidden (*haram*). Our conscience is from the heavens; it is always right. There is no such thing as a sick conscience, but sometimes we put such a heavy load on it that we are unable to hear its cry. Therefore, we must make an intention to always listen to our conscience. If we do this, Allah will give our conscience more power. Our conscience gives us good signs; do not try to fight against it. Do not try to justify bad actions. It is wrong. When Allah is not pleased with a man's actions, he makes all favors for that man forbidden, *haram*, in this life and in the next.

Do not imagine that the Lord Almighty is waiting for your prayers, your fasting, your covering your heads or your dressing in Islamic clothes, no. He is looking to your hearts to see if they contain an atom's weight of sincerity, and only if He finds that sincerity does He accept anything from you. None of your actions are, of themselves, pleasing to your Lord if they are not motivated by sincere intentions.

---

[54] Surat al-Hadid, 57:4.

Reaching to Unity

Grandshaykh once spoke to me about Jafar as-Sadiq ﷺ from the Naqshbandi Golden Chain. He was a descendant of the Prophet ﷺ. When he worshipped he was absent from himself, going into the Divine Presence. The value of worship is in that Presence. As much as you are with yourself, you are far away from genuine worship; you are a servant to yourself. Being absent from yourself means coming to Unity, *tawhid*. When you are present in the Divine Presence, all powers are present with you. There is no heedlessness; you do not forget anything. When you are with your ego, you may forget something in the prayer. The purpose of all worship is only to make you absent from yourself and present in the Divine Presence. As much as you are with yourself, there is no genuine unity.

The Heart's *Dhikr*

Once, daily, you must listen to your heart's *dhikr*. When you listen, you can hear your heart saying, 'Allah, Allah.' This is an important *wird*, more important than the tongue's *dhikr*. This gives concentration to the whole body. The best time to do this is after midnight, at tahajjud (before the dawn). First pray two prayer cycles (*rak'ats*), then sit and listen to your heart's *dhikr*. Your concentration will grow from this point to where that *dhikr*, the remembrance of your Lord, will be with you 24 hours a day. I am giving you permission; it means to take that 'electricity' from the center that the Grandshaykhs are opening for us. When my Grandshaykh gave me permission, he was opening, from his heart to my heart, such a power.

Allah Is the Main Power Station

Allah says that He has all power, and that His servants are powerless. Only Allah has Absolute Power, and only He gives power to the whole universe. Divine power is within everything that is in existence. Allah is the main power station for all creatures. If you know this, you know that as much as you are powerless, you must ask from your Lord.

Therefore, the Prophet ﷺ asked his Lord, "O my Lord, do not leave me to myself, my *nafs*, for even the blink of an eye. If you leave me to myself, I will perish." He was asking for divine help and power every moment, in all conditions throughout his life.

He often said that he was only a powerless servant and completely dependent upon his Lord; and when he said this, the Lord Almighty gave him from His Absolute Powers, saying, "For as much as you are admitting your own powerlessness, that much power We will give to you." All divine help and support comes most often to those who are weak in this world, more than to those who appear powerful. As much as you are in need, as much as you are opening to Allah, help is coming. If you do not feel in need of your Lord, you will be left to yourself, and you will perish.

The Power of the Shaykh

The Holy Prophet ﷺ prayed, *Allahumma, la takilni ila nafsi tarfat 'aynin.* "O Lord, do not leave me to my ego even for the blink of an eye."[55]

If you are with your ego, it cuts you off from others, and then you are alone with the ego. To feel and think that you are alone makes you depressive; it destroys the personality, and you are in a helpless situation. Loneliness is the beginning of difficulties and suffering, physically and spiritually. If you are alone, you are unable to think clearly and realize the needs of other people. If you are speaking to people, and you are not with your shaykh, then you are like a blind man throwing stones, unable to reach your target.

Therefore, you must ask, "O my shaykh, I am asking to be with you. You are with me, but I am not with you. I will try to be with you."

If these two currents meet, the power will run. The more you are able to concentrate on his being with you, the more power reaches you from his side. If you are wholly with him, then he is in you, and you are your own shaykh.

That is the meaning of "being with your shaykh." His power will surround you as much as you are with him, and then you should reach to unlimited power, because the shaykh is connected to the Prophet ﷺ, and the Prophet ﷺ is in the Divine Presence.

---

[55] Al-Hakim, an-Nisa'i and al-Bazzar.

Be with your shaykh, and you will not lose power, knowledge, wisdom, patience, or your life, because everything is with him. You are never alone, not even in deserts or on seas, even if you were the only human being on earth. You will be most powerful among people; and even if the whole of humankind was coming against you, you would not fear, because you are connected to the real power station. If anyone were to touch you, he would fall down.

The fact that this power exists makes our life easy and safe. There is no need to fear if we concentrate on our shaykh. However, if we forget him, hopelessness and depression, suffering and fear may come to us. Therefore, take him with you, wherever you are going. Then he will lead and guide you in everything. Then you will understand what it means to be with the Prophet ﷺ, to be with Allah. You will experience *fana* (annihilation). You will vanish, and He will appear in you.

Those are the people about whom the Prophet ﷺ said, "When you look to them, you look to Allah." If you are with your shaykh, Satan will never conquer your heart. He cannot enter because your shaykh is there with you. May Allah make it easy for us to be with one of His servants who is in the Divine Presence. Fatiha.

Heart Connection

Anytime you lose control over yourself, or you are in a difficult situation, you can be in contact with my heart immediately. If you just think about me there will be a relationship with me, and I will look to you. That connection will cause a power to run quickly between us, and you will be protected. It is like putting a plug in the socket, to connect with electricity.

The Secret Power of *Bismillah*

All power is from the Lord Almighty, and we must always ask for His support, because we are in need, we are weak ones.

the Lord Almighty ordered His Beloved Prophet, Prophet Muhammad ﷺ, to inform his Community that anything that is not begun with His holy name - *Bismillahi 'r-Rahmani 'r-Rahim—"in the name of God, the Compassionate, the Merciful,"*—will never be supported by Allah; it means it will never give fruit, and it must fail. If you say Allah's holy name, you will take benefit from that action, and any harm that may be in it will leave you. Whoever is feeling weak should say it, and power will come to his physical body and to his heart.

The *bismillah* is the most important key for opening all treasures in the heavens and on earth, and for opening all forms of knowledge. The Lord Almighty has put three thousand of His Holy Names in it: 1000 Names that are known only to the angels, 1000 names known by the prophets, 999 Names contained in the four Holy Books[56], and His Greatest Name. All of these Names are contained in the *bismillah.*

Whoever is able to reach to the secret power of the *bismillah* is dressed in miraculous powers. We, as servants of Allah, should say it at least 100 times daily. If a person continues for forty days, he should find some power, some changes in himself, especially if he says it one thousand times between Fajr and sunrise. From unseen worlds (*malakut*) beautiful views will appear to him. According to the thickness of the veils of his heart, from once over forty days, up to seven times over forty days, there should be an opening. If not, it means that his heart is too occupied with *dunya*, and he should try to put *dunya* last, and then try again. It is a rule that cannot be wrong. Even in one day it may be opened, because it is so powerful.

Every time you say *Bismillahi 'r-Rahmani 'r-Rahim,* it means that you are remembering the Lord, "O My Lord, I am remembering You!" Then Allah says, "O My servant, I am remembering you!"

Do not forget! If you forget, you will be forgotten.

[56] The Old Testament, the New Testament, the Psalms, and the Qur'an.

7. Divine Guidance

Istikhara: Asking for Guidance

If you are in doubt about something, whether it is the right thing to do or not, if it is according to Allah's Will or not, you can ask about it in the following way anytime:

Take a shower, with hot or cold water. You must be in a silent place. Give your greetings to Allah, your Lord. Then sit and say, "O my Lord, I am intending something, and I am asking for my will to follow Your Will. Give me the right sign for this purpose."

You will be given a green or a red light. You must take this seriously. Then it is impossible to do this and not to get an answer. This is a form of seeking Divine Guidance, *istikhara.* Anybody may do it. There is free permission to ask for everybody, who is interested to know, if they are acting according to their Lord's Will.

You must not ask about something that is already clear, and the direction has already been shown. In that case, you must accept whatever it is, and there is no need to ask about it.

It is best is to do this exercise before going to bed. Pray two cycles *rak'ats*, ask, and then go to bed without talking to anyone.

Genuine Inspirations

In order to distinguish genuine inspiration from stray thoughts and the whisperings of Satan, wait and see whether that inspiration recurs or not. Divine inspiration will come to your heart repeatedly. If evil whisperings do persist, it will become clear that they are not good by a kind of disturbance you feel in your heart. If it is an inspiration, there is never going to be doubt in your heart. You will find absolute satisfaction. If it is from the ego, your conscience will not be at rest.

From Heart to Heart

In our *tariqah*, what is the method of fighting the ego? It is to become accustomed to doing everything with permission of the shaykh, especially concerning marriage, divorce, and long journeys; and it is best to consult him in every important matter.

We possess a "walkie-talkie," and we can send waves from heart to heart. If you know the wavelength you can tune in, because a genuine shaykh must send. According to a disciple's station, a genuine shaykh can send him those waves. At the first station, the shaykh's presence comes to the heart of the disciple. At a more advanced stage, the disciple may actually feel the shaykh by his side and perceive his breathing. The final and most advanced stage is when the spiritual power of the shaykh dresses itself on the disciple, so that he 'becomes' the shaykh for a certain time.

Ears of the Heart

Knowledge comes in two ways. One is by listening from outside and using that in directing oneself on a way. But some knowledge comes from the heart, and this is more powerful in pushing one towards his target. In other words, if a command comes from outside, the ego does not take care to keep it, but when it comes from yourself, it has more effect. The ego never likes to be commanded, but if it is coming from the heart, you see it as honorable.

You may listen to so many lessons, but really you are waiting for that command to come from yourself. Correct and divine guidance come with the second way. The *awliya* may speak, but they also send inspiration to hearts. The *murshid* may teach by inspiration. Then one thinks about the knowledge coming, "I am thinking this." The more we are purified, the more divine wisdom waves can be caught by our hearts' ears.

The Prophet ﷺ said that if man can keep his heart pure, and worship sincerely for forty days, then he may catch divine wisdom in his heart and may speak wisdom, which is the essence of knowledge.[57]

---

[57] Al-Muttaqi al-Hindi's *Kanz al- 'Ummal.*

Meetings for The Sake of Allah

Allah's hand is over a congregation, *jama'at*; if they are meeting for worship, there will be divine assistance for those people. If they are going to do something according to our Lord's order, they will be under the guard of Allah. If they are going to do something according to the advice of the Prophet ﷺ, they will be under the guard of the Prophet ﷺ.

Whenever any group of our brothers or sisters meet for the sake of Allah, joining their hearts to the hearts of the masters of this Way, that meeting will attain the level of an association with the shaykh. In such a meeting, such a power descends on the hearts of the attendees that even the deepest roots of hidden idolatry, of ego worship, can be pulled out. Such an assembly is more beneficial than years of supererogatory worship.

Do not think that the only beneficial meeting is the one where the shaykh is physically in attendance. When our brothers or sisters meet, one of them must be the channel for inspiration to come from the shaykh: one must speak and the others listen; one must take from the shaykh and the others take through him from the shaykh.

In this way all the meetings of our brothers and sisters are blessed. If more than one person speaks, or if there are arguments and contention, then there will be no spiritual power in that meeting, and hearts will be left cold.

Real Life Comes from Divine Love

All souls are calling "O our Lord, save our souls!" They feel as if they are in Hell. Humankind is in need of spiritual food. It makes their faces bright and their hearts full of light, peace comes to their minds, and their spirits open towards the heavens. Contentment is dressed on their physical beings.

Sufi ways are spiritual ways, the ways to the heavens. If you like, you may follow them, so that your soul is in Paradise before you die. Then dying will only be like a change from one place to another, so easy, opening a door and being welcomed.

Divine Light: Food for the Soul

The prophets brought *Nur*, divine lights for our souls, which go through the hearts of people. Souls can only be fed by divine lights. There is no need for eating and drinking; their food is lights. Everyone's soul is in need of divine light. If they are not asking for light today, they will ask for it tomorrow, or next month, next year or on their last day in *dunya*. This is important. Souls are thirsty for the stream of Divine Lights, and if there are no lights, there is no love. If Allah's Beauty Oceans cannot be seen, no love comes to His servants. Souls know that, and therefore they are asking for those divine lights. Through them, those oceans become visible, and souls should be satisfied.

Love Is Life and Light

Try to give more time every day to prayers and *dhikr*. Angels glorify their Lord without tiring; it is their food. So the power of one angel is more than the power of all humankind. It is a special power. Spiritual people, prophets and saints, have it.

Glorifying the Lord gives you energy and peace, more power and support, and more love for Allah. Real life comes from that Divine Love. When there is no love, there is no life. The *awliya* say that whoever does not have that love is like a dead body walking on earth. Love is life and light, and the more we have of it, the more our life will be complete and full of pleasure.

The Power of Divine Love

In their inner life, people are in need, and with their souls, they are in contact with my soul, so they come to me. I am doing nothing with my followers. I am only sending divine power to them without their knowing, which works through their personalities without harming them. The benefit of a master is that he takes away bad characteristics in order to give good attributes to people. It needs a gardener to look after fruit trees and make them perfect.

Masters give perfection to *mureeds*. To be like the master is the perfection of a disciple. As much as you imitate your master, following him step-by-step, you are going to be on the same level, but you are an imitation of him. I am making *mureeds* follow me through their hearts, with love. I am not using force, but the power of love.

The Heart Is for Allah Alone

The Lord Almighty asks of His servants to worship with *ikhlas* (sincerity, purity). He asks for pure worship, which means to have a pure heart, a heart that has nothing in it but its Lord.

Each of us knows which side is not true, or which of his characters is not good. We must strive to have pure hearts. That is jihad: to fight with one's bad characters and change them into good ones.

Everything that occupies your heart and keeps you from your Lord makes your heart impure. You must try to keep everything away from your heart, but Allah. We say that the heart is for Allah alone. Man is created for the love of the Lord Almighty. Any time you put your love in this *dunya*, it will be wasted. If you put your love with Allah, with the Prophet ﷺ, with your shaykh, or with your fellow believers, you may find that love here and in the Hereafter; it is never going to be wasted. Love is the most precious, most valuable, most expensive thing that the sons of Adam have been given.

8. *Jihad Al-Akbar*: The Greatest Struggle

The Base of Faith

The base upon which faith is built, the spirit of faith *(ruh al-iman)* is to carry everything that you do not like, and to be patient with those you do not like. For as many people as there are on this earth, such is the number of different characters and abilities, and you must carry them all. Whenever you are carrying other people, you get more power, more strength for your faith. The genuine power of faith is to remain unchanged in the face of trials.

In our times, the sign of good character, and the highest degree of *jihad al-akbar* (the greatest struggle) is to carry other people's bad characters and to tolerate them.

We have not been ordered to refuse people, but to make them more pleased. We are living in a time when people may say anything and everything; you must be patient with them, and excuse them, always without fighting. You must know that people are ill with their egos. If you are claiming to be doctors, you must excuse them. If you are on the way of prophets, you must help them and be tolerant of them. This is the highest degree of good manners.

You must not forget a goodness that has been done to you. If someone does goodness for you, and afterwards you become displeased with that person over something he said or did, your displeasure, your forgetfulness of that person's good deed toward you is from bad character. You will be like a cat. You may give it meat one hundred times; but if you leave it just once, that cat will make objections and complaints to Allah, saying, "He left me hungry!"

It is good manners not to argue with people, even if you know that you are in the right. Arguing extinguishes the faith.

Who is a genuine Muslim? One who does not harm anyone, either with his hands or with his tongue. People are safe from him. This is a wide entrance to Islam, and it is for all people.

The Sixth Pillar of Faith

Whenever something is wrong in a person, everything around him appears wrong to him. When he is right within himself, the world appears right to him. The world is created perfectly by our Creator. If something appears wrong to you, you must ask yourself, "What is wrong in me that I see this as wrong? O my *nafs*, you are wrong!"

This is the highest degree of faith, and the highest degree of belief in the goodness of the Creator. Allah is not creating anything wrong or imperfect. At the essence of everything, if we could but see it, there is perfection. Until we behave correctly with our Lord, it is impossible for our actions, our family, and our neighbors to behave correctly with us. It is impossible to find a better situation than that which exists today, for those who are ready. You cannot wish for things to be as they used to be, nor for the way that they might be. The conditions that we are in now are perfect, most suitable for us. The Lord Almighty is giving as much of His mercy as we need, as much as we are able to carry.

Genuine faith is like that: to believe that all actions, whether from goodness, or from badness, are from the Lord Almighty. If we believe this, we must be patient with each other's actions. Allah is trying our faith, each of us with others.

The Prophet ﷺ said, "People will deal with you according to your actions." If you are good and someone intends you harm, Allah will defend you. You must be honorable to all, good, respectful, merciful, generous and think well of all. We must be patient with all people because we believe that no one comes to us without our Lord's Will. Therefore, there is no enmity in Islam. We have been ordered to do goodness. Anyone can return goodness for goodness; but only a few people can return goodness for badness.

O My Lord, I Am in Need of Your Mercy!

A genuine servant to his Lord knows that all the goodness that he has is a mercy from his Lord, guiding him to his Lord's way. He knows that but for his Lord's mercy, he would not be praying, fasting, making *dhikr*, and so forth. So, when he comes to his Lord's Presence, he says, "O my Lord, I am standing in Your Divine Presence, and my hands are empty. I am in need of Your mercy always. Give me more mercy, O my Lord."

A genuine servant of the Lord is not asking anything from Him. He says only, "May you be pleased with me, O my Lord."

Some *awliya* are too ashamed to ask anything from their Lord, because they see that they are in endless need of Him. They say, "O my Lord, You know best what I need from Your Mercy. My needs are endless. Fulfill my needs, O my Lord, as You know."

Achieving the Station of Contentment: How to Control Anger

Who is the happiest person in this life? Who is the most satisfied? He who is satisfied with that station in life in which his Lord put him. It is the station of contentment, to look at everything and see that it is most suitable for him, and for all. You must say, "This situation is most suitable for me because my Lord put me in this situation. If it were no good for me, He would not have put me in it." We must believe that the Lord Almighty desires goodness for us, always.

Do not be a teacher to Allah. He knows best, and you do not know anything. Do not make any objections for anything; you are servants, you are slaves to Him, and He is Governor, Absolute King of the Universe.

You must know that all actions, all events, are not going to happen as we like them to happen. Nothing happens, no one can be as we like them to be; it is impossible. When you know this, you may keep yourself far away from anger, because anger is the result of thinking that you can have everything as you want it to be.

With Pleasure, O My Lord!

If a man is going to do anything, worship or any other action, it must be done voluntarily and gladly. If he is not pleased with that action he must not do it, for there will be no good result from it. If there is no pleasure in it for you, there will be no pleasure in it for the Lord Almighty. For worship, it is important to realize that we are speaking of the soul's pleasure. When we are worshipping, our *nafs* is not pleased, but our souls are. We must look to the pleasure of our soul.

Actions may be easy or difficult. What is the secret? For the one who finds an action easy, it is because it gives him pleasure, while the one who finds it difficult, it is because he is forced to do it. Easy actions make people happier, while difficult actions make people unhappy.

There Is No "Empty Time"

Everything that is going to happen in this life has a fixed time. Every event has an appointed hour. If we know that all events will come in their appointed time, we will be at rest and patient; patience shows the perfection of Man, and a strong faith.

If we can take wisdom from every event, then we will be strong in faith. We will get more power to receive divine knowledge. Allah orders us to look deeply into each thing, into each event, to find a secret wisdom that gives it value. If you look deeply, you will taste.

Everything must be in its time. You cannot put it out of its time, because every moment is occupied. You cannot find time that is 'empty'. Therefore, in our *tariqah* there is no delaying of actions. Actions must be done in their times. As the Lord Almighty says, "For prayer there is a special time and order." This is a sign for us. Asking us to delay our actions comes from the ego, *nafs*. Our *nafs* is very lazy; it does not like to move, and therefore it wishes to delay everything. To our *nafs*, it seems easy to say, "I'll do it tomorrow." It is always looking for an escape from serious actions because it only likes to play.

9. Characteristics of Allah's Servants

Tawbah: Repentance

Tawbah (repentance) means not to listen to one's four enemies: the *nafs* (ego), *hawa* (vain desires), *dunya* (physical world) and Satan (Satan). Man may agree with his Lord or with his four enemies. If a man is asking to return to his Lord, he must be in rebellion against those four enemies, and not listen to their orders.

Be Acceptable in the Divine Presence

Our Grandshaykh described how a dervish may be acceptable as a servant to the Lord Almighty.

"He must have one character from each of three animals," he said.

"From the donkey, he must be able to carry burdens with patience and without objection. Unless he can do this, he will be unsuccessful, because without patience one cannot carry the responsibilities of life.

"From the dog, he must learn faithfulness to his master. If the master tells the dog to stay somewhere until he returns, that dog will stay, even until death. If the owner beats it and chases it away, the dog will still return, with its tail wagging, when its master calls.

"Finally, when a man looks at a pig, he must know that his *nafs* is dirtier and filthier than a pig. The dirt of pigs is external; it comes from eating dirty things. But the *nafs* is dirty inside. Its dirt comes from fighting with its Lord. A perfect man must have such a character that he will accept whatever dirt is thrown on him, whether by words or by actions, knowing that his *nafs* is dirtier."

These three characteristics give a man rest and satisfaction in his heart. Only in this way can he reach happiness in this life. These are the characteristics of prophets and saints.

Twelve Good Characteristics in Dogs

Our Grandshaykh said, "There are twelve good characters in dogs that you may also find in prophets and *awliya*. They are:

- They do not forget those who have done goodness to them.
- They are patient and always grateful for everything that they are given.
- They are not angry with their owners, even if they are beaten and sent away.
- If their owners call, they return with their tails wagging.
- They are humble.
- They are obedient.
- They are truthful.
- They are trustworthy, and make good friends.
- They are loyal, always remaining with their owners and never turning traitor.
- They are satisfied with small things; they are *zahid*, not looking to anything from this *dunya*.
- They have nothing from this world, they have no place for themselves. They may sleep anywhere, and if someone throws stones at them, they quickly get up and go somewhere else.
- They are very light sleepers, not sleeping too much, and they awaken quickly.

These twelve attributes belong to prophets and saints. If one possesses them, he is a *wali*."

God Tests His Servants

The Lord Almighty tries His servants to see if they are patient. We must remember this so that when an event comes to test our patience we will remain firm. We must keep "patience at the first blow," we must keep our faith, then our power will grow and the power of our enemies will decrease. Our real enemy is our own ego. In the great battle against our ego *(jihad an-nafs)* the angry man will lose and the patient man gains.

Will You Be Patient?

Patience is fighting everything that the *nafs* likes, and is of three types:

1. Patience with physical discomforts, such as getting up on cold mornings for prayer, having cold water for washing, waiting in line, being uncomfortable during illness, completing difficult tasks, and so forth. To remain patient and steadfast in your worship despite these difficulties is very valuable in the sight of Allah.
2. Even more valuable is the patience to refrain from forbidden things. A Hadith says, "To live as a servant and to keep away from forbidden things is more valuable than the worship of all the angels, men and jinn throughout the ages."
3. The third type of patience is the best of all: to be patient with those who trouble you. The Holy Qur'an says, *"We are trying some of you with others of you."*[58]

Patience is the most necessary thing in the life of humankind. If you have patience, all goodness is with you. Allah's Eyes are on you. Will you be patient?

The Sign of Spiritual Health

People with good character are healthy in their spiritual lives. From the amount of a person's complaining, you may know how much of bad characteristics are left with him. When you finish all your complaining, you may know that you are healthy; no more bad character.

This is important, because a person with a good character, if he has no complaint and he has patience, that means he has genuine faith. When you can escape the pull of your bad characteristics, there are no troubles for you either, whether in this life or in the Hereafter. You must remember that this is going according to your Lord's Will. This is the key, the medicine for that illness.

---

[58] Surah Muhammad, 47:4.

You must say, "Why am I complaining, when the Lord Almighty has ordered this thing to happen?" When you remember this, you will be satisfied with His Will and agree with it.

The Secret Unbeliever

If one is not aware that Allah's Eyes are on him or her, everywhere, all the time, he or she is not a *mu'min* (believer). You must imagine in your heart that Allah's eyes are upon you. If you forget this, you will be absent from your Lord, and present with your ego. The best actions come by keeping this in your mind.

If a man is doing an action that is not pleasing to Allah, His Prophet ﷺ or His *awliya*, it means that he is considered a "secret *kafir*," a secret unbeliever. We have been ordered to clean ourselves of both evident and secret *kufr* (disbelief). Therefore, you must be careful about your openly visible acts as well as your secret acts. You must keep a balance with you with which to weigh your actions. You must look at each action that you do, or are about to do, and make sure that it will be pleasing to Allah, His Prophet ﷺ and the *awliya*. When you know that that action will bring pleasure to your Lord, the Prophet ﷺ and the *awliya*, you may do it. If not, you must leave it.

If a man balances his actions in this life, there will be no balancing for him on Judgment Day.

The Prophet ﷺ said, "It is more lovely to Allah if a man sits for an hour thinking and weighing of his actions, than if he prays for seventy years!"[59]

This is because you may erase your seventy years of worship with an act that Allah is not pleased with; but if you weigh of that action first, with your mind, you may be able to leave it, and escape its harm.

---

[59] As-Sufuri in *Nuzhat al-majalis*.

That Which Does not Concern You

The Prophet ﷺ said, *min husni Islami al-mar' tarkahu ma la ya'nih* – 'From the excellence of a person's Islam is to leave that which does not concern him."[60]

Ma la ya'ni means, "That which does not concern you." You must not speak of or act on that which does not concern you. If a man takes care of his speech, keeping his tongue, the Lord Almighty gives divine wisdom to his tongue so that he speaks only truth and righteousness. To speak of that which does not concern you makes your faith weak. When you leave this bad habit, your faith becomes stronger. You cannot know what concerns you or not, save through your inspirations. Then you may know very well what is yours or not.

Are We Building or Destroying?

The spirit of all acts of worship consists of three points:

- To keep your tongue from all prohibited speaking, speaking only good words, not bad.
- To keep your eyes from looking at prohibited things, dirty places, and actions.
- To keep all your organs from prohibited acts, be they through listening, walking, touching, thinking, or having bad intentions.

Without keeping your eyes, tongue, and organs from what is prohibited, you cannot take any benefit from your good actions. Like when you are planting something, you must keep it safe and protect it from harm. We must know what we are doing. Are we building or destroying? Every prohibited action destroys our building; destroys our physical and spiritual bodies.

[60] Tirmidhi, *Musnad* Ahmad, Ibn Majah.

First Fight Yourself

To be able to put one's organs under one's will is the mark of a genuine servant of Allah. If a man cannot do this, he is the servant of his ego, *nafs*. You must be able to advise yourself, before you may advise others. If your self accepts being under your command, then other people may accept being under your command.

This is the way of prophets and *awliya*. First they fight themselves, and then they look after other people. When they speak, their words have an effect upon those who listen. If a person listens, it is impossible for him not to take benefit from the words of a Prophet or a Saint. He may take power to control his *nafs* and go on the right way. It is not enough to say, "I am Muslim," and recite the declaration of faith, *shahadah*. You must try to keep your organs far from all actions that are not for us, far from forbidden things, *haram*.

The Bond of Divine Love

The Lord is One. He created all of us and planted His Divine Love in the very yeast of our being. You must know that, although that love may be temporarily covered, it is running through our hearts as a river runs to an ocean. It may manifest only as temporary human love, it may even seem to disappear completely, like a river that flows under a mountain, only to re-emerge on the other side. But there can be no doubt that our Lord has placed in every heart a current that flows irresistibly to His love oceans in the Divine Presence.

Allah says, "O My servants, as I have given you of My Divine Love, so have I given it to all creation; so spread your love to everyone, that you may be in harmony with My Will."

To perceive the beauty in all creation you must transcend outward forms and shapes and pass to meanings, eternal spiritual realities, as forms are limited and limiting, whereas spiritual realities are oceans, endless oceans of contentment. To arrive at those oceans will bring you inner peace.

There are levels of love along the way. Their quality is different, according to their nearness to the goal, the Absolute love oceans of our Lord. When one has reached that goal, he may take any amount of harm from others and still love. He may say, "I love you for the sake of my Lord, not for any other reason. That love will never change or diminish, as no matter what you do your Lord's love is with you, and therefore I love you, too."

We are trying to reach that point, but it is difficult. We are tested, and that is an opportunity for us to advance. Holy people have advised us that rather than avoiding all ill-mannered and badly-educated people, we should mix with them and establish contact with them, that they may benefit, that we may test ourselves, and thereby gain.

The holy masters have promised me that whoever sits with me and listens with his heart full of love, being receptive to Divine Love, must come to the same level: their hearts must open to Divine Love. The masters are not going to abandon us, and we are not going to turn from them, as our hearts have been bound with the strongest bond: the bond of Divine Love, that strongest relationship that exists between the Creator and His creatures.

If the love that is with me was only transitory love, you would not sit with me for even one moment. But the love that is with me is genuine, permanent and divine; and I extend rays of it to your hearts in my association to awaken permanent love in you. This is a love that will blossom in your hearts. I am asking permission from my Lord to spread His permanent Divine Love to the hearts of all people. The time is approaching when we hope that permission will be granted.

Ya Wadud: The Fountain of Divine Love

All creatures appeared through Allah's Divine Love. He loved them and they appeared; therefore, everything in existence carries its share of Divine Love in it. The electrons of atoms turn around the nuclei with the speed of light, because they are alive with the Divine Love Power that their Lord has granted them.

It is Allah who, through His Holy Name, Ya Wadud, the All-Loving, gives His Divine Love to everything in the Universe. Those electrons spin at such high speed around the nuclei because they are drunk with Divine Love. That is how the influence of that love is manifested by them. Through the Divine Name, al-Wadud, genuine, never changing, permanent love is granted to us by the Lord. When we recite the supplication "ya Wadud," we are opening ourselves up to that Divine Love, asking our Lord to awaken that unlimited and eternal love. I have been ordered to teach and advise people to call on our Lord, saying "ya Wadud," as this will enable the sincere to attain genuine love of their Lord the Lord Almighty and to love everything around themselves for the sake of the Creator who loves all of His creation.

This love is the essence of all success in the way of spiritual purification. To realize that love, to come into contact with the Divine Love Oceans, is the challenge and fulfillment of human existence. We seek to awaken permanent love. Practices, prayers and rules are of no use in our time without that love, because the ego easily attaches itself to practices and uses them, so that they serve our vanity.

Everyone has a circle of friends, relations, and acquaintances. Starting from those closest to us, our wives or husbands, parents and children, brothers and sisters, we must be generous in giving of our permanent love, making peace with them. Giving of our permanent love is the most important practice for our time. The lower self of Man, the selfish ego, never wants to give permanent love to anyone except himself. But Man has been created to love all creation, as he represents his Lord on earth and has the greatest reservoir of Divine Love with him. He can be a great means of expression for that Divine Love in this world, a fountain of love that every creature may drink from.

The Need of a Divine Mirror to See Oneself

Do you think that we came from the Divine Presence with our whole originality, our whole personality? Never. We are like one ray of the sun. We are, in our originality, in reality, still in the Divine Presence. Not moving, out of time and space there is no movement. We are continuously worshipping, always in the Divine Presence for service. Here, in this life, there is only one ray from that timeless 'sun' for us. We are here for a little time only.

Prophets have come to us to open that door through which we can look at our realities in the Divine Presence. Step-by-step, if you are following in their footsteps, it will open for you to look at yourself, to know yourself. We do not know ourselves; we need a divine mirror to look in to see ourselves. You are asking why we come to this life: it is to be witnesses of ourselves. We have been sent to attain perfection, to look at ourselves and say, "We are something also." I cannot give more than this description until you taste it for yourself. When you taste, you will know.

May Allah grant us to taste. *Bi hurmati'l-habib.* Fatiha.

10. Appendix of the Naqshbandi Essentials

Following are the spiritual practices of the esteemed Golden Chain of masters of the Most Distinguished Naqshbandi Order *(silsilat adh-dhahabīyati 'l-āhlu'l Khwajagān mina 'ṭ-ṭarīqati 'n-Naqshbandīyyati 'l-ʿaliyyah).*

Tawassul: Plea For Acceptance

Yā sayyid as-sādāt wa nūr al-mawjudāt, yā man hūwa al-malja'u liman massahu ḍaymun wa ghammun wa alam. Yā aqrabu 'l-wasā'ili ilā-Allāhi taʿalā wa yā aqwā 'l-mustanad, attawasalu ila janābīka 'l-ʿaẓam bi-hādhihi's-sādāti, wa āhlillāh, wa āhli baitika 'l-kirām, li-dafʿi ḍurrin lā yudfaʿu illā bi wāsiṭatik, wa rafʿi ḍaymun lā yurfaʿu illā bi-dalālatika bi Sayyidī wa Mawlāy, yā Sayyidī yā Rasūl Allāh, yā man arsalahu 'llāhu Raḥmatan li 'l-ʿālamīn: Al-Fātiḥah.

O, master of the masters and light of the existence. O, refuge of the one who has been struck by afflictions, distress and pain. O, closest of means to approach Allah. O, most powerful of supports. I entreat your mighty presence by means of these masters, and the people of Allah, and the honored members of your family, for the removal of harm that cannot be removed except by your intercession, and the lifting of affliction that cannot be lifted except by your guidance, by my master and lord, O my master, O Prophet of Allah, O Mercy to the worlds. Al-Fatiha.

- *Allāh, jalla jalālahu subḥāna wa taʿala*
- *Sayyidinā Nabī Muḥammad, Rasūl Allāh* ﷺ
- *Sayyidinā Abū Bakr as-Ṣiddīq* ؓ, *Khalīfatu Rasūl Allāh* ﷺ
- *Salmān al-Fārsī* ؓ
- *Qāsim bin Muḥammad bin Abū Bakr aṣ-Ṣiddīq* ؓ
- *Imām Jʿafar aṣ-Ṣādiq*
- *Sulṭān al-ʿArifīn Abū Yazīd Ṭayfūr al-Bistamī*
- *Abu 'l-Ḥasan al-Kharaqānī*

- *Abū ʿAlī Aḥmad al-Farmādī*
- *Khwājā Abū Yaʿqūb Yūsuf al-Ḥamadāni*
- *Abu 'l-ʿAbbās Sayyidinā 'l Khiḍr* ﷺ
- *Imām al-Khatm: Khwājāʿ Abd al-Khāliq al-Ghujdawānī*
- *Khwājā ʿArif al-Rivgarī*
- *Khwājā Maḥmūd Faghnawī*
- *Khwājā ʿAzīzān ʿAlī ar-Ramitānī*
- *Muḥammad Bābā as-Samāsī*
- *Khwājā Sayyid Amīr al-Kulālī*
- *Imām aṭ-Ṭarīqah wa Ghawthu 'l-Khalīqah Khwājā Bahā'uddīn Naqshband Muḥammad al-Uwaysī al-Bukhārī*
- *Khwājā ʿAlā'uddīn al-Attar al-Bukhārī*
- *Khwājā Yaʿqūb al-Charkhī*
- *Khwājā ʿUbayd Allāh al-Aḥrār*
- *Sayyidinā Shaykh Muḥammad Zāhid al-Bukhārī*
- *Sayyidinā Shaykh Darwīsh Muḥammad*
- *Mawlāna Aḥmad Khwājā Amkanākī*
- *Sayyidinā Shaykh Muḥammad al-Bāqī billāh*
- *Mujaddidu'l Alfi 'th-Thāni Imām Rabbāni Aḥmad al-Fārūqī as-Sirhindī*
- *Shaykh Muḥammad Maʿṣūm as-Sirhindī*
- *Sayyidinā Shaykh Sayfuddīn ʿArif bin Muḥammad Maʿṣūm*
- *Sayyidinā Shaykh as-Sayyid Nūr Muḥammad*
- *Sayyidinā Shaykh Shams ud-Dīn Ḥabībullāh Jān-i-Janān*
- *Sayyidinā Shaykh ʿAbd Allāh ad-Dahlawī*
- *Sayyidinā Shaykh Khālid Ḍiyā' ud-Dīn al-Baghdādī*
- *Sayyidinā Shaykh Ismāʿīl ad-Dāghestanī*
- *Sayyidinā Shaykh Khāṣ Muḥammad ad-Dāghestanī*
- *Sayyidinā Shaykh Muḥammad Effendī al-Yarāghī*

- *Sayyidinā Shaykh Sayyid Jamāluddīn al-Ghumūqī al-Ḥusaynī*
- *Sayyidinā Shaykh Abū Aḥmad aṣ-Ṣughūrī*
- *Sayyidinā Shaykh Abū Muḥammad al-Madanī*
- *Sayyidinā Shaykh Sharafuddīn ad-Dāghestānī*
- *Sulṭān al-awlīyā Shaykh ʿAbd Allāh al-Fā'iz ad-Dāghestānī*
- *Mawlāna wa Ustādhinā as-Sayyid Shaykh Muḥammad Nāẓim ʿAdil al-Ḥaqqānī an-Naqshbandī*

Qaddas-Allāhū taʿalā arwāḥahumu 'z-zakīyya, wa nawwar Allāhū taʿalā aḍriḥatahumu 'l-mubāraka, wa aʿād-Allāhū taʿalā ʿalaynā min barakātihim wa fuyūḍātihim dā'iman wa 'l-ḥamdulillāhi Rabbi 'l-ʿālamīn, al-Fātiḥā.

May Allah sanctify their pure souls and illuminate their blessed graves, may He return to us from their blessings and overflowing bounty, always; and all praise belongs to Allah, the Lord of the Worlds. Al-Fātiḥā.

Bay'ah: The Pledge Of Allegiance (Initiation)

Bayʿah is a conscious confirmation of the connection between the master and his disciple. The disciple "allows" his shaykh and master to work with him, accepting to be his student and follower, for the sake of his spiritual progress toward his destination.

The disciple puts his hand in the hand of the master or on his stick or coat. Other people can also be connected by putting their right hand on the right shoulder of the person in front of them. The master says:

Aʿudhū billāhi min ash-Shayṭān-i 'r-rajīm, Bismillāhi 'r-Raḥmāni 'r-Raḥīm. Inna'lladhīna yubayʿūnaka innamā yubayʿūna'llāh, yadu'llāhi fawqa aydīhim, fa man nakatha fa innamā yankuthu 'ala nafsi, wa man awfa' bimā 'ahada 'alayu'llāh fasayuʿtihi ajran ʿaẓīma.

Allāh Hū, Allāh Hū, Allāh Hū, Ḥaqq

Ḥasbī-Allāhu wa niʿm al-wakīl, lā ḥawla wa lā quwwata illa billāhi 'l-ʿAlīyyi 'l-ʿAẓīm.

Raḍīnā billāhi Rabban, wa bi 'l-Islāmi dīnan, wa bi sayyidinā Muḥammadin ṣalla-llāhū ʿalayhi wa sallam rasūlan wa nabīyyan, wa bi Mawlanā Shaykh Muḥammad Nāẓim al-Ḥaqqānī shaykhan wa murshidan.

Ila sharafi 'n-Nabīyy Muḥammadin ṣalla-llāhū ʿalayhi wa sallam wa ilā arwāḥi jamīʿi 'l-anbīyā'i wa 'l-mursalīn wa khudamā'i sharāʿihim wa ila arwāḥi 'l-a'immati 'l-arbaʿah wa ila arwāḥi mashāyikhinā fi 'ṭ-ṭarīqati 'n-naqshbandīyyati 'l-ʿaliyyah khāṣṣatan ila rūḥi Imāmi 'ṭ-ṭarīqati wa ghawthi 'l-khalīqati Khwājā Baḥā'uddīn an-Naqshband Muḥammad al-Uwaisī 'l-Bukhārī wa ila ustādhinā wa ustādhi ustādhinā Khwājā ʿAbd al-Khāliq al-Ghujdawānī wa ila ḥaḍarati Mawlanā Sulṭānu 'l-awlīyā ash-Shaykh ʿAbd Allāh al-Fā'iz ad-Dāghestanī wa ila sayyidunā ash-Shaykh Muḥammad Nāẓim al-Ḥaqqānī Mu'ayyad ad-dīn wa ila arwāḥi sa'iri sādātinā waṣ-ṣiddiqīna al-Fātiḥā.

After the *bay'ah,* the initiate may also receive a new name from the shaykh. Every individual has been granted seven heavenly spiritual names, all of which are known to the shaykh. These names help and guide the *mureed* (disciple) on the way of personal development.

Rabitatu 'sh-Sharifa: Connection with the Shaykh

Our Grandshaykh Shah Naqshband said, "God looks at the hearts of His saints with His lights, and whoever is around that Saint will get the blessings of those lights. Whoever is initiated by us and follows and loves us, whether he is near or far, wherever he is, even if he is in the East and we are in the West, we nourish from the stream of Divine Love and give him divine light in his daily life."

The Prophet ﷺ said:

Tafakkur saʿatin khayrun min ʿibādati saba'īn sanatin.

Contemplation and meditation for one hour is better than seventy years of supererogatory worship.[61]

Make *ghusl* or *wudu,* and put on clean clothes if possible. Pray two cycles *(rak'ats)* of greeting for the ablution, *tahiyatu 'l-wudu.* Then sit down in a silent private place and face the *qiblah.* Close your eyes and try to stop all movements, thinking and wishing. Imagine yourself in the presence of your shaykh and him sitting in front of you. For that purpose, you can try to

---

61 As-Sufuri in *Nuzhat al-majalis.* Another version is: "Contemplation for one hour on the alteration of the night and day is better than eighty years of worship." (ad-Daylamī) Yet another version is related: "Contemplation for one hour is better than sixty years of worship." (Abu ash-Shaykh in his *Azamah*)

remember a moment you had with the shaykh that was pleasant or impressive to you, or use a picture of him to remember his face. Connect with him through your heart, turning in love towards him.

"Sincerity is to worship Allah as if you see Him; for even if you do not see Him, He sees you."

The shaykh is the representative of the Prophet ﷺ, who is *khalifatullah.*

Remember that the shaykh is always looking to us, that he is always with us, even though we may not be able to see, hear, or feel him. This is why we are not with him and forget him. Imagine yourself always in his presence, he being at your side, no matter what you do. This will protect you from misbehaving.

To connect with the shaykh, read three times Sūratu 'l-Ikhlāṣ and one time Sūratu 'l-Fātiḥa. Dedicate them to Prophet Muhammad ﷺ and to the soul of our Grandshaykh, Abd Allah ad-Daghestani. Then ask for Mawlana Shaykh Nazim's presence.

You can imagine the heart of the shaykh like an Ocean of Divine *Fa'iz* (blessings), and your own heart like a vessel that is being filled with that *fa'iz* running from the shaykh's heart to yours. Alternatively, you can imagine your shaykh covering you like a tent under which you are sitting; on all sides Divine *Fa'iz* is raining down. You can also imagine yourself swimming in the Ocean of the shaykh's heart, like a fish or a drop of water.

If you experience interference or disturbance by other images, open your eyes quickly. The images will disappear and then you can continue to concentrate. If disturbing thoughts are coming to you, recite the following 100 times or more, until they disappear:

lā ḥawla wa lā quwwata illa billāhi 'l-ʿAlīyyi 'l-ʿAẓīm.

There is no power nor strength with me except that which is coming from Allah, the most High, the Magnificent.

Aʿudhū billāhi min ash-Shayṭān-i 'r-rajīm,

I seek refuge in Allah's Presence from the cursed Satan.

Grandshaykh Shah Naqshband said, "The seeker in this way must be busy in rejecting evil whisperings and the ego's demands, either before they reach him, or after they reach him, but before they control him. A seeker who does not reject them until after they reached him and controlled him cannot get any fruit, because at that time it is impossible to take the whisperings out of the heart."

Silent *Dhikr*

When practicing the silent dhikr of the heart, place your tongue on the upper palate and the teeth flush on top of each other.

To deepen the concentration while listening to the heart's dhikr you can imagine the Name of Allah made of light being engraved on your heart.

Naqsh: Engraving

Everything has been created for Man except for his heart. The heart is for Allah Alone, so that He can make it His Throne. The *naqsh* (engraving) is Allah's stamp, or seal on the heart. During the training in the Naqshbandi Order, Allah's Name is being perfectly engraved in the heart of the seeker or disciple.

The Strong Intention

Our Grandshaykh, Abd Allah ad-Daghestani said, "I will teach you a way to approach me quickly. Whenever you do your prayers, make dhikr, read Qur'an, anything that you are doing, make the following intention:

Nawaytu 'l-arbāʿīn, nawaytu 'l-ʿitikāf, nawaytu 'l-khalwa, nawaytu 'l-ʿuzla, nawaytu 'r-riyāḍa, nawaytu 's-sulūk, lillāhi taʿala fī hādhā 'l-masjid.

I am intending the forty days, retreat, seclusion, abstinence, contentedness, following in obedience, fasting, for the sake of the Lord Almighty, in this mosque.

Worshipping with this intention is deducted from the forty days of seclusion, which are obligatory for a Naqshbandi disciple.

Grandshaykh Shah Bahauddin Naqshband said, "Intention, *niyyat*, is very important. It consists of three letters: *nūn,* which represents *Nūr Allāh* (light of God); *ya*, which represents *yad Allāh* (hand of God); and *ha*, which represents *hidayatu'llāh* (the guidance of God). *Niyyat* is the breeze of the soul, coming from the unseen world, not from the material world."

On the way of Truth, *ṭarīq al-ḥaqq*, two methods are being used: *tariqahs* follow either the *ṭarīqi nafsānī*, through which the *nafs* (ego) is educated for the soul to be saved, or *tariqi rūḥānī*, through which the *rūḥ* (spirit, soul) is purified.

The *ṭarīqi nafsānī* is heavy. You must always do the opposite of what your ego wants from you. It is a big fight. The *tariqi rūḥānī* is easy. In the Naqshbandi Way, you can use the best of everything under the condition that you also do your best in worshipping Allah. On this Way, first of all the spirit or soul is purified, with no regard to the ego. After the *ruh* has found its original attributes, the ego, willingly or unwillingly, must follow the *ruh* and obey its orders.

The shaykh opens—from his heart to the heart of the disciple—a spring of *fa'iz*, (divine blessings), from the Divine Oceans of *fa'iz*. He increases the love for Allah in the heart of the disciple, and in this fire of Divine Love all worldliness is burned. Through the *fa'iz* the heart is cleaned, then the state of the disciple changes. It is through the *baraka* and the spiritual power of the shaykh that the disciple progresses from the lowest level or state of his soul to the highest.

There are two beings in the Children of Adam (humanity) which are always fighting: the *rūḥ ḥayyanīyya,* which is always rebellious and against Allah, and the *rūḥ sulṭānīyya*, which is always obedient to Allah and finds its pleasure in worshipping Allah. If the lower self is absolutely in control, one's characteristics can be worse than a wild animal's. If the higher self is absolutely in control, one's characteristics can be better than those of the angels. To reach the state known as *insān-i-kāmil*, a perfected human being, one must undergo training at the hands of a perfect master, because the *nafs* (ego) must develop.

The Seven Levels

There are seven levels of evolution of the self (*nafs*):

Nafs al-Ammara

The ego is in full power. The lower self always prompts one to disobey Allah and to do evil, bad actions and the gratification of animal lust. One is pleased with oneself and full of bad characteristics.

Nafs al-Lawwama

The conscience is awakened, and the self accuses one for listening to one's ego. One repents and asks for forgiveness, but falls back into bad behavior.

Nafs al-Mulhimma

One becomes more firm in listening to one's conscience, but is not yet surrendered.

Nafs al-Mutma'inna

One is firm in faith and leaves bad manners. The soul becomes tranquil and at peace.

Nafs ar-Radiya

One is pleased with whatever comes from Allah and does not live in the past or future, but in the moment. One thinks always: *'Ilāhī Anta maqsūdī wa riḍāka maṭlūbī*—My God, You are my goal and Your Pleasure is what I seek.' One always sees oneself as weak and in need of Allah.

Nafs al-Mardiya

The two souls, the animal soul (*rūḥ ḥayyānī*) and the human soul (*rūḥ sulṭānīya*) have made peace. The person is soft and tolerant with people and has good *akhlāq* (conduct).

Nafs as-Safiya

One is dressed in the attributes of *insān-i-kāmil,* the perfected human, who is in a state of complete surrender and inspired by Allah, in full agreement with the Will of Allah.

Five Stations of the Heart

There are five stations of the heart: heart, *Qalb;* Secret, *Sirr;* Secret of the Secret, *Sirr as-Sirr;* Hidden, *Khafā,* and Most Hidden, *Akhfā.* The first station Satan can enter. The second station belongs to the shaykhs of the forty *tariqahs*; the third only to the shaykhs of the Naqshbandi *tariqah;* the fourth to the Holy Prophet ﷺ and the fifth to the Lord Almighty.

Seclusion and Retreat

The true seclusion is to empty the heart of everything except Allah and to be alone with the One you love. It means to leave one's own self behind like a snake sheds its skin. Shah Naqshband said that it is impossible to reach the love of the *Āhlu'llah*, the People of God, until you come out of yourself.

In seclusion, one isolates and secludes oneself from anyone other than Allah and disconnects from the materialistic life for the sake of being able to remember Allah all the time and be with Him. It is a period of training in the Sufi *tariqah* during which the lower self is deprived of even the permitted enjoyments of normal Muslim life; it involves fasting, absolute seclusion, increased prayer and remembrance of Allah and reduced sleep. The disciple must fight his ego with great courage and determination, because the ego will give him intense difficulties.

According to Abu 'l Hasan ash-Shadhili, there are ten benefits from seclusion:

- Safety from all misconduct of the tongue.
- Safety from all misconduct of the eyes.
- Safety of the heart from displays of pride and other bad characteristics.
- Safety from the company of evil people.
- Safety of the ego from falling into bad manners.
- It lifts you to a state of asceticism.
- It enhances your time for *dhikr*.
- It enhances your time to meditate, to take account of yourself and to focus on reaching the Divine Presence.
- It enhances the sweet taste of worship and supplication to the Divine Presence.
- It brings peace and satisfaction to the heart.

Grandshaykh Abd Allah ad-Daghestani said that to enter seclusion is like planting a seed in the ground. It vanishes from the materialistic side of this life for the love of Allah and the benefit of other human beings, and it begets fruit. Like this, you must cut yourself off from the materialistic life, forsake your ego, and vanish into nothingness to exist only in the Presence of Allah. Being alone with your Lord, you make a connection to your ultimate reality, by fitting that image you wear here to its original in the Divine Presence. It is in seclusion that the eyes of the heart open and the heart finds the satisfaction and happiness it seeks.

Expression of the Goal

Ilāhi anta maqsūdī wa riḍāka matlūbī! lā ma'būda ill-Allāh, lā maqsūda ill-Allāh, lā mawjūda ill-Allāh!

O Allah, You are my goal and I am seeking Your satisfaction! There is nothing worthy of being worshipped except Allah, there is no other destination except Allah, there is no other existence except through Allah!

Primary Rules of the Naqshbandi Sufi Way

The following rules demonstrates the goals of *tariqah*, as formulated by our glorious guides (may Allah sanctify their souls!) Shaykh Abdul Khaliq Ghujdawani and Shah Bahauddin an-Naqshband.

Hosh Dar Dam: Conscious Breathing

You must not inhale or exhale heedlessly. Every breath should be associated with an awareness of the Divine Presence, because it then is alive and connected with the Divine Presence.

Through the breathing of the creatures, the sound of *Huwa* of the Divine Name of Allah is made, and this is a sign of the Unseen Divine Essence in all creatures, pointing to the Uniqueness of Allah.

Nazar Bar Qadam: Watch Your Step

While walking, you must watch your steps keeping the eyes on your feet, and not look here and there. Unnecessary sights and images create veils on the heart, which block the light of the Divine Presence. Do not let your ego distract you, but move steadfastly toward your goal: the Divine Presence. That is the way of the Holy Prophet Muhammad ﷺ: to look solely for the Divine Presence.

Safar Dar Watan: Journey Homeward

There are two kinds of travel. The first is the external journey, the travel from one land to another searching for a perfect guide to take and direct you to your destination. This enables you to go on the second journey that is internal. It involves a journey from human to angelic attributes. You must leave bad characteristics, move to the praiseworthy ones, and throw all worldly desires out of your heart to purify it. Through unceasing effort, especially during the early stages of the Way, the mirror of the heart must be polished. *Ad-dawāmu-tawfīq* (Perseverance brings success).

Khalwat Dar Anjuman: Solitude in the Crowd

It means to be outwardly with people while remaining inwardly with Allah. Your outward activities must not affect your inward state of remembrance of Allah, the *dhikrullāh.*

There are also two kinds of seclusion. The external seclusion requires that the seeker must seclude himself in a private place and stay there by himself, pray and make dhikr. He chains his ego, his external senses, for his internal senses to become free to reach to the heavenly realm. This will bring him to the state of internal seclusion, wherein his heart is present with his Lord and absent from the creatures while remaining physically present among them. In the state of dhikr, the manifestation of the Divine Presence envelops him. When it overcomes him, it makes him unaware of all but his Lord.

The Prophet said ﷺ, "I have one face which is facing my Creator, and I have another face which is facing the creation."

Yad Kard: Remembrance, Mentioning

Remember Allah both with the tongue and with the heart, by making loud and silent *dhikr*. The *dhikr* by negation and affirmation is *la ilāha ill-Allāh.* The *dhikr* of the Name of Allah's Essence is *Allāh, Allāh.* By these forms of *dhikr*, you deny everything in this world and affirm the existence of the Lord Almighty only. This brings you into the Divine Presence of Allah.

Baz Gasht: Returning

The Holy Prophet said, *Ilāhi anta maqsūdī wa riḍāka matlūbī:* "O Allah, You are my goal and Your satisfaction is what I seek."

To utter this phrase every now and then during the *dhikr* helps you to expel all thoughts from the heart, and to open yourself to the awareness of the Oneness of Allah, until you reach the state that wherever you look you will see the Absolute One.

Return to Allah by complete surrender and submission to His Will, and complete humbleness in giving Him all praise. The seeker cannot come to the Presence of God in his dhikr except by the help, support, and the permission of Allah. It is really Allah, the One, who is reciting the dhikr through that person.

Shaykh Abu Yazid al-Bistami said, "When I reached Allah I saw that His remembering of me had preceded my remembrance of Him."

The Holy Prophet ﷺ said, "We did not remember You as You deserve to be remembered, O our Lord!"

Nigah Dasht: Attentiveness

Watch your heart during the contemplation. It will help you to prevent egoistic and evil thoughts from entering it. Bad inclinations keep the heart from joining with the divine.

Yad Dasht: Recollection

Always safeguard your heart with *dhikr* and be in permanent awareness of the Divine Presence. Then you will also discard thoughts from your imagination, keeping and affirming only the genuinely truthful thoughts.

Wuqufi-i-Zamani: Awareness of Time

You must be aware of how you spend your time, as it is said, "The Sufi is the son of his time." Stop every now and then in your activities to remember Allah.

Spend time making your only goal the arrival at the station of Divine Love and Divine Presence. You must become aware that Allah witnesses the smallest detail. Make an account of your actions and intention each night and analyze them. If they are good, and if you were in Allah's Presence, thank Allah for them. If they are bad, and you were in the presence of your ego, you must repent and ask Him for forgiveness.

Wuquf-i-Adadi: Awareness of Numbers

Count and be aware of the exact number of repetitions comprising the silent *dhikr* of the heart, to secure your heart from bad thoughts and to deepen the concentration. The pillar of *dhikr* through counting is to bring the heart into the Presence of the One who is mentioned in that *dhikr* and to realize the creation's need of Him.

Wuquf-i-Qalbi: Awareness of the Heart

The heart is the center of power. All thoughts and inspirations, good or bad, are felt and appear inside the heart, circling and alternating, moving between light and darkness. *Dhikr* is required to control and reduce that turbulence of the heart.

The state of awareness of the heart is the state of being present in the Divine Presence in such a way that you do not see other than Allah.

You can form a mental picture of your heart with the name *Allah* engraved on it, to emphasize that the heart has no consciousness or goal other than Him.

Wazifa: The Basic Exercise of the Naqshbandi Order

This basic exercise recited once in twenty-four hours.

ADAB		
Practice	***Dhikr***	**Meaning**
3 x Bear witness – *shahāda*	*ash-hadu an lā ilāha ill-Allāh wa ash-hadu anna Muḥammadan ʿabduhū wa rasūluh*	I testify that there is no god but God, and I testify that Muhammad is the Servant and Messenger of God.
70 x Seek forgiveness – *istighfār*	*Astaghfirullāh*	God forgive me.
Seek blessings	Sūratu 'l-Fātiḥah With the intention of sharing in the manifestations (*tajalliyyāt*) and Divine Favors sent down when it was first	

	revealed in Makkah al-Mukarrama.	
	Āman ar-rasūlu (Quran 2:285-6)	Below
	Sūratu 'l-Ikhlāṣ	Below
7 x	Sūratu 'l-Inshirāḥ	Below
	Sūratu 'l-Falaq	Below
	Sūratu 'n-Nās	Below
9 x *kalimah*	*Lā ilāha illa-Allāh*	There is no god but God
	Lā ilāha illa-Allāh Muḥammadun Rasūl Allāh	There is no god but God, Muhammad is the Servar and Messenger of God.
10 x Prayers on the Prophet - ṣalawāt	*Allāhumma ṣalli ʿalā Muḥammadin wa ʿalā āli Muḥammadin wa sallim*	O God send blessings an peace upon Muhammad the family of Muhamma
Gift the reward - *Ihdā*	Below	Below
Recitation	Sūratu 'l-Fātiḥah with the intention of sharing in the *tajallīyāt* and divine favors sent down when it was revealed for the second time in Madinat al-Munawwarah.	Below
3 x	*Allāh Hū, Allāh Hū, Allāh Hū, Ḥaqq*	
	WIRD	
Practice	***Dhikr***	**Meaning**
1500 x Remember God - dhikr	*Allāh, Allāh*	God, God.
100 x Prayers on the Prophet - ṣalawāt	*Allāhumma ṣalli ʿalā Muḥammadin wa ʿalā āli Muḥammadin wa sallim*	O God send blessings an peace upon Muhammad the family of Muhamma
Recitation of Qur'ān	One *juz'* (1/30) of the Qur'ān	

-or- 100 x	-or- Sūratu 'l-Ikhlāṣ	
Dalā'il al-Khayrāt -or- Prayers on the Prophet-Ṣalawāt 100 x	One chapter -or- *Allāhumma ṣalli ʿalā Muḥammadin wa ʿalā āli Muḥammadin wa sallim*	O God send blessings and peace upon Muhammad and the family of Muhammad

Ayah Āman ar-rasūlu (Qur'an 2:285-286)

Āmana ar-rasūlu bimā unzila ilayhi min Rabbihi wa 'l-mu'minūn. Kullun āmana billāhi wa malā'ikatihi wa kutubihi wa rusulihi lā nufarriqu bayna āḥadin min rusulihi wa qālū samʿinā wa aṭʿanā ghufrānaka rabbanā wa ilayka 'l-maṣīr. Lā yukallif-ullāhu nafsan illa wusʿahā. lahā mā kasabat wa ʿalayhā māktasabat. Rabbanā lā tū'ākhidhnā in nasīnā aw akhṭānā. Rabbanā wa lā taḥmil ʿalaynā iṣran kamā ḥamaltahu ʿalā alladhīnā min qablinā. Rabbanā wa lā tuḥamilnā mā lā ṭāqata lanā bihi wʿafu ʿanā waghfir lanā warḥamnā Anta mawlānā f'anṣurnā ʿalā l-qawmi 'l-kāfirīn.

Āmana billāhi ṣadaq-Allāhu 'l-ʿAẓīm. Subḥāna Rabbika Rabbi 'l-ʿizzati ʿamā yaṣifūn wa salāmun ʿalā 'l-mursalīn wa 'lḥamdulillāhi Rabbi 'l-ʿalamīn.

The Messenger believeth in what hath been revealed to him from his Lord, as do those who have faith. Each one (of them) believeth in God, His angels, His books, and His apostles. "We make no distinction (they say) between one and another of His apostles." And they say: "We hear, and we obey: (We seek) Thy forgiveness, our Lord, and to Thee is the end of all journeys." On no soul doth God place a burden greater than it can bear. It gets every good that it earns, and it suffers every ill that it earns. (Pray:) "Our Lord! Condemn us not if we forget or fall into error; our Lord! Lay not on us a burden like that which Thou didst lay on those before us; Our Lord! Lay not on us a burden greater than we have strength to bear. Blot out our sins, and grant us forgiveness. Have mercy on us. Thou art our Protector; Help us against those who stand against faith."

Dedication (*Ihda*)

Allāhumma balligh thawāba mā qarā'nāhū wa nūra mā talawnāhū hadīyyatan wāṣilatan minnā ila rūḥi Nabīyyīnā Sayyidinā wa Mawlānā Muḥammadin ṣalla-llāhū ʿalayhi wa sallam. Wa ilā arwāḥi ikhwānihi min al-anbiyā'i wa 'l-mursalīn wa khudamā'i sharāʿihim wa ila arwāḥi 'l-a'immati 'l-arbaʿah wa ila arwāḥi mashāyikhinā fi 'ṭ-ṭarīqati 'n-naqshbandīyyati 'l-ʿaliyyah khāṣṣatan ila rūḥi Imāmi 'ṭ-ṭarīqati wa ghawthi 'l-khalīqati Khwājā Baḥā'uddīn an-Naqshband Muḥammad al-Uwaisī 'l-Bukhārī wa ḥaḍarati Mawlanā Sulṭānu 'l-awlīyā ash-Shaykh ʿAbd Allāh al-Fā'iz ad-Dāghestanī wa sayyidunā ash-Shaykh Muḥammad Nāẓim al-Ḥaqqānī Mu'ayyad ad-dīn wa sa'iri sādātinā waṣ-ṣiddiqīna al-Fātiḥā.

O God! Grant that the merit of what we have read, and the light of what we have recited, are (considered) an offering and gift from us to the soul of our Prophet Muhammad, and to the souls of the prophets, and the saints; in particular the soul of the Imām of the ṭarīqat and arch-Intercessor of the created world, Baḥā'uddīn an-Naqshband Muḥammad al-Uwaisī 'l-Bukhārī, and our venerable teacher and master, the Sultan of Saints, our Shaykh ʿAbd Allāh al-Fā'iz ad-Dāghestanī, and our master Shaykh Muḥammad Nāẓim al-Ḥaqqānī Mu'ayyad ad-dīn, and to all our masters to the souls of the preceding masters and veracious ones. *Al-Fātiḥah*

Duʿa (Personal prayer, supplication), Al-Fātiḥah.
This presents the reward of the preceding recitations to the Prophet ﷺ and to the shaykhs of the Naqshbandi Order with the intention of sharing in the manifestations, tajallīyāt, and Divine favors sent down when it was revealed for the second time in Madinat al-Munawwarah.

Suratu 'l-Fatiha, 1

Aʿudhū billāhi min ash-Shayṭān-i 'rrajīm, Bismillāhi 'r-Raḥmāni 'r-Raḥīm. Alḥamduli'llāhi Rabbi'l ʿAlamīn, ar-Raḥmāni 'r-Raḥīm, māliki yawmi 'd-dīn. Īyyāka naʿbudu wa īyyāka nastaʿīn. Ihdinā ṣiraṭa'l-mustaqīm, ṣirāta 'lladhīna anʿamta ʿalayhim, ghayri 'l-maghḍūbi ʿalayhim wa lā 'ḍ-ḍālīn. Āmīn.

All praise is due to Allah, the Lord of the Worlds; the Merciful, the Beneficent; Owner of the Day of Judgment. You alone do we worship and You alone do we ask for help. Guide us on the straight path, The way of those on whom Thou hast bestowed Thy Grace, those whose (portion) is not wrath, and who go not astray. Amen.

Suratu 'l-Inshirah, 94

Alam nashraḥ laka ṣadrak, wa waḍa'na 'anka wizrak, alladhī anqaḍa ẓahrak, wa rafa'na laka dhikrak, fa inna ma'a 'l-'usri yusra, inna ma'a 'l-'usri yusra, fa idhā faraghta fanṣab, wa ila Rabbika farghab.

Have We not widened your breast, and taken the burden off your back, and have We not raised your name in fame? So truly, with every hardship comes ease, with every hardship comes ease, so when you are free from your immediate task turn to your Lord and worship Him.

Suratu 'l-Ikhlas, 112

A'udhū billāhi min ash-Shayṭān-i 'rrajīm, Bismillāhi 'r-Raḥmāni 'r-Raḥīm. Qul Hūwa 'llāhu Āḥad. Allāhu 'ṣ-Ṣamad, lam yalid wa lam yūlad, wa lam yakun lahu kufuwan āḥad.

Say, He is Allah the One, Allah, the eternally independent. He has not given birth to anyone nor was He born from anyone, and none is like Him.

Suratu 'l-Falaq, 113

Qul: A'udhū bi Rabbi 'l-falaq, min sharri mā khalaq, wa min sharri ghāsiqin idhā waqab, wa min sharri nafathāti fi'l 'uqad, wa min sharri hāsidin idhā ḥasad.

Say, I am taking refuge in the Lord of the dawn from the evil that He has created, from the evil of the darkness after sunset, and from the evil of those who blow on knots making magic, and from the envier when he is envious.

Suratu 'n-Nas, 114

Qul: A'udhū bi Rabbi 'n-nās, maliki 'n-nās, ilāhi 'n-nās, min sharri 'l-waswāsi 'l-khannās, alladhī yuwaswisu fī ṣudūri 'n-nās, mina 'l-jinnati wa 'n-nās.

Say, I seek refuge in the Lord of humankind, the King of humankind, the God of humankind, from the evil of the whisperer, who whispers into the breasts of Man evil about the jinn and humankind.

Salat Tunjina: Prayer of Relief

This is a very important supplication, which seeks goodness and relief from problems. It is recited each day, forty times after Salat al-Fajr:

Allāhumma ṣalli ʿalā Muḥammadin ṣalātan tunjīnā bihā min jamīʿi 'l-ahwāli wa 'l-āfāt, wa taqḍī lanā bihā min jamīʿi 'l-ḥājāt, wa tuṭahhirunā bihā min jamīʿi 's-sayyi'āt, wa tarfaʿunā bihā ʿindaka ʿalā 'd-darajāt, wa tuballighunā bihā aqṣā 'l-ghāyāt min jamīʿi 'l-khayrāti fi 'l-ḥayāt wa baʿd al-mamāt.

O our Lord, grant Your blessings to our master Muhammad (and the family of our master Muhammad), blessings with which we may be saved from all adverse conditions and misfortunes, with which all our needs may be fulfilled, with which we may be cleaned from all sins, with which may be raised to high spiritual ranks, and with which we may attain the best of all kinds of goodness in this life and the Hereafter.

Ḥasbī-Allāhu wa niʿm al-wakīl (3 times), niʿm al-Mawlā wa niʿm an-Naṣīr, ghufrānaka rabbanā wa ilayka 'l-maṣīr.

Allah is sufficient for me and the Best to arrange all my affairs. He is the best Lord I can have and the best One to advise me. I am asking Your forgiveness, O our Lord, and to Your Presence we return.

Optional Recitations

10 times (to 100) *Bismillāhi 'r-Raḥmāni 'r-Raḥīm*

10 times (to 100) *Alḥamdulillāhi*

10 times (to 100) *Lā ilāha illa-Allāh*

10 times (to 100) *Allāhumma ṣalli ʿalā Muḥammadin wa ʿalā āli Muḥammadin wa sallim*

10 times (to 100) *Allāh, Allāh*

10 times (to 100) *Yā Wadūd*

10 times (to 100) *Ḥasbī Allāhū wa nʿima 'l-wakīl*

10 times (to 100) *lā ḥawla wa lā quwwata illa billāhi 'l-ʿAlīyyi 'l-ʿAẓīm.*

The Five Pillars of Islam

Islam is the outward surrender to the orders of Allah, and accepting/upholding the five pillars of Islam, which are:

- *Shahāda*—Testification of Faith. Declaring there is no God save the One True God, the Lord Almighty, and that Muhammad ﷺ is the Messenger of Allah.
- *Ṣalāt*—Prayer. To pray the ritual prayer facing Makka five times a day at the prescribed times and upholding its prerequisites.
- *Ṣawm*—Fasting. To fast the month of Ramadan, abstaining from all food, drink and carnal pleasures from pre-dawn until sunset.
- *Zakāt*—Charity. To give 2.5 percent of one's wealth annually to the poor.
- *Hajj*—To offer pilgrimage to Makka in the prescribed manner at least once in a lifetime, provided one possesses the material means and health.

The Six Pillars of Faith

Īmān is a stage when true faith has entered the heart. The six pillars of *īmān* are:

- Belief in the One God (Allah).
- Belief in the angels.
- Belief in the holy books that God sent to humankind through His prophets.
- Belief in the prophets of God.
- Belief in the afterlife, Heaven and Hell.
- Belief in predestination, that God has decreed everything that occurs in this world, regardless of whether it appears to be good or bad.

Glossary

Adab: Protocols established by example of Prophet Muhammad; etiquette; good manners; proper behavior.

Adhān: The Arabic call to prayer recited loudly to call worshippers to the five daily prayers, observed since the earliest days of Islam. The congregational prayer cannot be observed without *adhān*. Translation: "Allah is the Greatest; I bear witness that there is no God other than the True God Allah, I bear witness that Muhammad is the Messenger of Allah; Come to the prayer, come to true success; Allah is the Greatest, there is no God but Allah."

Āhlu 'l-Ḥaqq: People of Truth.

Āhlullāh: People of God (Allah).

Awlīyā: Friends of God (Allah); saints.

Allāh: Arabic name for God. Derived from "*al-ilāh*" (the God).

Baraka: Divine blessing; benediction; Abundant and continual good; spiritual emanation of holy people, places and objects.

Barzakh: The world in which the deceased exist while awaiting Resurrection and Judgment Day.

Fitna: Dissension; discord, strife, affliction.

Ghusl: A ritual shower performed after sexual intercourse, upon the cessation of menstruation, and by the mother forty days after childbirth.

Ḥadīth: Prophetic tradition; a record of the legal judgments and examples of Prophet Muhammad.

Ḥalāl: Permissible, lawful, legitimate, according to the divine law *(Shari'ah)*.

Ḥarām: Forbidden, unlawful, prohibited either because of sacredness or the harm it will generate; actions which fall outside the limits of *Shari'ah*.

Hawā: Vain desires, fancies, inclinations; distractions and idle or vain thoughts that keep one from reality and worship.

Himmah: Energy, vigor; ambition, resolution, determination, zeal, aspiration.

Islām, Imān, Iḥsān: The three levels of faith.

Iḥsān: The highest spiritual state and level of faith. The Holy Prophet ﷺ said that *iḥsān* means to worship as if you see Allah in front of you, for even if you do not see Him, He sees you.

Ikhlāṣ: True sincerity; purity of intention. A very high state of devotion.

Islām: The outward surrender to the orders of Allah, accepting the five pillars of Islam.

Jāhilīīyya: The "days of ignorance" refers to the pre-Islamic era during which the Arabs worshipped idols, followed superstitions, and practiced female infanticide.

Jihād al-Akbar: "The greater holy war" that is fought against one's ego. Without achieving discipline over the lower self, one cannot perfect personal conduct or faith.

Jinn: Created of smokeless fire, beings that coexist in the world with humans and angels. Both believers and unbelievers are found among the jinn.

Ka'bah, Baytullāh: The holy house of God in Makka. Muslims worldwide direct themselves in their prayers toward the Ka'ba as their central focal point, known as *Qiblah.* When visiting the Ka'ba, Muslims perform the rite of circumambulation, emulating the angels who circumambulate the Throne of God in Heaven. Ka'ba

Kāfir: Anyone who disbelieves or rejects divine truth brought from God by the prophets and saints. Unbelief: *kufr.*

Khidmah: Service for the shaykh, his followers, human beings and all creatures.

Muftī: Official expounder of Islamic Law, and highest religious authority in the land, usually appointed by the head of state.

Murīd: A disciple of the Sufi way, who submits himself to the care and spiritual training of a Sufi shaykh.

Murshid: Guide, advisor, instructor. One who leads another to the right way; a Sufi shaykh.

Muslim: One who surrenders to the will and commands of God.

Nasīḥa: Sincere advice. The Holy Prophet said, *Ad-dīnu nasīḥa*: "Religion consists of sincere advice."

Qur'ān: (Koran); lecture; recitation; the holy book of the Muslims, revealed over 23 years exclusively to Prophet Muhammad. It is a revelation from Allah, the Lord of the Worlds, carried down from Heaven by archangel Gabriel to the heart of Muhammad ﷺ, and passed on by the Prophet to humans and jinns. The Qur'an is the eternal speech and guidance of God transmitted in the Arabic language, with special mystical power. While translations are useful, they do not stand in the place of the original Arabic, neither in prayer nor spiritual benefit. Since its revelation, not one letter has been changed; it has been preserved in its original form for fifteen centuries.

Rak'at: One cycle of the ritual prayer (*Ṣalāt*) which consists of either two, three, or four *rak'ats*.

Saḥāba: The 124,000 Companions of Prophet Muhammad who lived in his presence; the major transmitters of his example.

Ṣalāt: ritual prayer, obligated for Muslims to practice five times per day.

Shari'ah: The Canon Law of Islam, the totality of God's commandments relating to the activities of humans; the indispensable basis for religious life. *Shari'ah* and *Ḥaqīqat* (the mystical reality) form a correlated pair, giving to Man the possibility of unfolding his potential to the highest degree.

Shirk: Polytheism; ascribing partners unto God. Hidden *shirk* is, for example, the worship of money, lusts, reputation, etc.

Sunnah: The practice and way of Prophet Muhammad that encompasses everything from his manners, pronouncements, advice, and rulings.

Tabi'īn: The three subsequent generations after the *Saḥāba*; those who were instructed directly by the *Saḥāba* (companions of the Prophet).

Tajallī: Spiritual emanations and manifestations.

Walī: a friend of God; a saint. (plural: *awlīyā*; feminine: *walīya*)

Wuḍu: Ritual ablution; prerequisite to prayer and reading the Qur'an; one offers his or her intention and then rinses the hands, mouth, nostrils, face, forearms, head, ears, back of neck and feet. Ablution is voided upon going to the toilet, passing wind, becoming angry or sexually aroused, and after sleep.

Other Titles from

THE ISLAMIC SUPREME COUNCIL OF AMERICA

THE PRACTICE OF SUFI MEDITATION AND THE HEALING POWER OF DIVINE ENERGY

By Dr. Hedieh Mirahmadi and Sayyid Nurjan Mirahmadi
ISBN: 1-930409-26-5, Paperback. 200 pp.

For those who have reached a level of understanding of the illusory nature of the world around us and seek to discern the reality that lies behind it, Sufi meditation, *muraqabah*, is the doorway through which we can pass from this realm of delusion into the realm of realities.

Through meditation the seeker has a means to return to his or her perfected original self. *Muraqabah* is the most effective method for advancing in spiritual degrees. It is in fact a migration from one's self to God. Through meditation higher states of consciousness are attained, and the connection to the seeker's true inner self is established, built-up and maintained, providing the practitioner with a lifeline to the Divine Presence. This book presents the spiritual background behind the practice of meditation, then takes the reader step-by-step, through the basics of spiritual connection based on the ancient teachings of the Naqshbandi Sufi masters of Central Asia.

IN THE SHADOW OF SAINTS

Sufi Discourses of Shaykh Muhammad Hisham Kabbani

ISBN 1-930409-32-X, Paperback, 108 pp.

A wise person once said, "Our bodies come new, but our spirits are ancient. When packaged together, this strange combination can work miracles." With today's global issues of violence, lack of racial and religious tolerance and the void of spiritual leadership, people are losing hope and falling away from the old establishments of faith, as they are constantly failing to offer solutions and peace of mind. That is one of the many reasons why people today are adapting the "new age" school of thought-seeking alternative means to find a light to guide them amidst the present spiritual darkness and material exuberance. But we are living in this moment, that of a new century and new generations.

Every generation is identified by its great thinkers, its great philosophers, its great leaders; those who enlighten that generation by their great service towards mankind, not only for their time, but for all to follow. Those auspicious personalities that transcend space and time become legends. They are heroes of the new age and we are living in the age of such new heroes. Shaykh Muhammad Hisham Kabbani is such a personality. He is a new type of teacher who teaches without teaching; a new age guru who melts hearts without holding a single session of Sufi gathering; a new age shaykh who inspires and illuminates the seeking heart without moving his lips.

PEARLS AND CORAL, I & II

By Shaykh Muhammad Hisham Kabbani

ISBN 1-930409-07-9, Paperback. 250 pp.
ISBN 1-930409-08-7, Paperback. 150 pp.

A series of lectures on the unique teachings of the Naqshbandi Order, originating in the Near East and Central Asia, which has been highly influential in determining the course of human history in these regions. Always pushing aspirants on the path of Gnosis to seek higher stations of nearness to the God, the Naqshbandi Masters of Wisdom melded practical methods with deep spiritual wisdom to build an unequalled methodology of ascension to the Divine Presence.

KEYS TO THE DIVINE KINGDOM

By Shaykh Muhammad Hisham Kabbani

ISBN 1-930409-28-1, Paperback. 140 pp.

God said, "We have created everything in pairs." This has to do with reality versus imitation. Our physical form here in this earthly life is only a reflection of our heavenly form. Like plastic fruit and real fruit, one is real, while the other is an imitation. This book looks at the nature of the physical world, the laws governing the universe and from this starting point, jumps into the realm of spiritual knowledge - Sufi teachings which must be "tasted" as opposed to read or spoken. It will serve to open up to the reader the mystical path of saints which takes human beings from the world of forms and senses to the world within the heart, the world of Gnosis and spirituality - a world filled with wonders and blessings.

THE SUFI SCIENCE OF SELF-REALIZATION

A Guide to the Seventeen Ruinous Traits, the Ten Steps to Discipleship and the Six Realities of the Heart

By Shaykh Muhammad Hisham Kabbani

ISBN 1-930409-29-X, Paperback. 244 pp.

The Sufi master Abu 'l-Hasan al-Kharqani asserted that the human state contains seventeen chief ruinous traits, each of which resembles a great tree, with main branches, smaller branches, twigs and leaves, all laden with various kinds of negativity. At the same time, human beings were granted six tremendous powers from the Divine: the power of attraction; the power of manifesting God's blessings; the power of intercession for those who oppress themselves; the power of directing the heart of seekers; the power of guidance; and the power to move in time and space. The path from submersion in the negative traits to the unveiling of these six powers is known as migration to Perfected Character. Through a ten-step program, the author--a master of the Naqshbandi Sufi Path--describes the science of eliminating the seventeen ruinous characteristics of the tyrannical ego, to achieve purification of the soul. The sincere seeker who follows these steps, with devotion and discipline, will achieve an unveiling of the six powers which lie dormant within every human heart.

Angels Unveiled: A Sufi Perspective

By Shaykh Muhammad Hisham Kabbani

KAZI Publications
ISBN: 1567445144, Paperback, 262 pp.

There are some books, like some people, whose words are so pure and clear they seep into your hear, spreading love and happiness, the light of the spiritual world. This is one of these. Both those who follow Islam and those unfamiliar with this Path, will find sweet comfort here, and the knowledge that at the core all paths to God lead to the one same shining goal." --Sophy Burnham

"The traditional Islamic universe is replete with angels who perform various functions in accordance with God's Command and the Noble Quran and Hadith speak often of the angels and their multifarious roles. At the time when interest in the angels is being aroused in the West once again, one cannot but welcome heartedly the appearnace of this book, which speaks with such traditional authority and clarity about angels in the Islamic cosmos and their role and function in various aspects of the daily life of Muslims." --Dr. Seyyed Hossein Nasr

---

CLASSICAL ISLAM

and the Naqshbandi Sufi Tradition

***Scholars in Islam* Series**

By Shaykh Muhammad Hisham Kabbani

ISBN 1-930409-10-9 (2004) Hardbound 950 pp.

Considered one of the most distinguished schools of Islamic spirituality, the Naqshbandi Sufi Order has an illustrious history that reaches back to the first days of Islam. Led by the shaykhs of the "Golden Chain," inheritors of the spiritual knowledge of the prophets and saints, since the time of Prophet Muhammad in 6th century Arabia, the Naqshbandi Order has played a pivotal role in the evolution of the Muslim world. It survived turmoil of past centuries to remain one of the few authentic mystical traditions that maintains a living link with its ancient past.

CLASSICAL ISLAM AND THE NAQSHBANDI SUFI TRADITION is the most detailed, authentic account of a Sufi order presented in the English language. Distinguished author, lecturer, and scholar, Shaykh Muhammad Hisham Kabbani, vividly narrates life stories that are intimately woven with landmark historical events. Bringing to bear his voluminous knowledge of Islamic jurisprudence combined with superlative storytelling, Shaykh Kabbani provides readers with a sumptuous feast, one that can be returned to again, not only for its comprehensive detail, but for inspiration and guidance in today's turbulent world.

THE NAQSHBANDI SUFI TRADITION GUIDEBOOK OF DAILY PRACTICES AND DEVOTIONS

By Shaykh Muhammad Hisham Kabbani

ISBN 1-930409-22-2, Paperback. 352 pp.

This book details the spiritual practices which have enabled devout seekers to awaken certainty of belief and to attain stations of nearness to the Divine Presence. The Naqshbandi Devotions are a source of light and energy, an oasis in a worldly desert. Through the manifestations of Divine Blessings bestowed on the practitioners of these magnificent rites, they will be granted the power of magnanimous healing, by which they seek to cure the hearts of mankind darkened by the gloom of spiritual poverty and materialism.

Includes the daily personal *dhikr* as well as the rites performed with every obligatory prayer, rites for holy days and details of the pilgrimage to Makkah and the visit of Prophet Muhammad in Madinah.

NAQSHBANDI AWRAD OF MAWLANA SHAYKH MUHAMMAD NAZIM ADIL AL-HAQQANI

Compiled by Shaykh Muhammad Hisham Kabbani

ISBN 1-930409-06-0, Paperback. 104 pp.

This book presents in detail, in both English, Arabic and transliteration, the daily, weekly and date-specific devotional rites of Naqshbandi practitioners, as prescribed by the world guide of the Naqshbandi-Haqqani Sufi Order, Mawlana Shaykh Muhammad Nazim Adil al-Haqqani.

THE APPROACH OF ARMAGEDDON? An Islamic Perspective

by Shaykh Muhammad Hisham Kabbani

ISBN 1-930409-20-6 (2003) Paperback 292 pp.

Expertly presented, this critically acclaimed book chronicles scientific breakthroughs and world events of the Last Days as foretold by Prophet Muhammad. A classical scholar from one of the Middle East's most prestigious religious schools, the author examines divine revelation and holy traditions about the Last Days, along with discoveries of modern science as foretold in Islam's holiest texts. Also included are often concealed ancient predictions of Islam regarding the appearance of the anti-Christ, Armageddon, the leadership of believers by Mahdi ("the Savior"), the second coming of Jesus Christ, and the tribulations preceding the Day of Judgment. The author weaves a fascinating mix of interpretations and detailed narratives of Prophet Muhammad, which provide a roadmap of the future and analysis of the past. Though terrifying in their import, we are given final hope of a time on earth filled with peace, reconciliation, and prosperity; an age in which enmity and wars will end, while wealth is overflowing. No person shall be in need and the entire focus of life will be spirituality." This unprecedented work is a "must read" for religious scholars and laypersons interested in broadening their understanding of centuries-old religious traditions pertaining to the Last Days.

MUHAMMAD: THE MESSENGER OF ISLAM

His Life And Prophecy

By Hajjah Amina Adil

ISBN 1-930409-11-7 (2002) Paperback 608 pp.

Since the 7th century, the sacred biography of Islam's Prophet Muhammad has shaped the perception of the religion and its place in world history. English biographies of Muhammad -- founder of the faith that currently claims 1.5 billion followers, roughly one-fourth of the world's population -- have characteristically presented him in the light of verifiable historical authenticity. MUHAMMAD: THE MESSENGER OF ISLAM goes one step further in skillfully etching the personal portrait of a man of incomparable moral and spiritual stature, as seen through the eyes of Muslims around the world. Compiled from classical Ottoman Turkish sources and translated into English, this comprehensive biography should be of interest to scholars of Islam and to all who seek to understand the essence of the faith, which is deeply rooted in the life example of its prophet. This esteemed biography not only details Muhammad's life, it also includes mystical secrets that Muslims believe were granted to the prophets who preceded him in the holy land and in other regions of the Middle East. This impressive biographical work deftly weaves quotes from authentic religious texts with ancient lore, resulting in a compelling, unforgettable read.

MY LITTLE LORE OF LIGHT

By Hajjah Amina Adil

ISBN 1-930409-35-4, Paperback, 204 pp.

My Little Lore Of Light is a children's version of Hajjah Amina Adil's four volume work, Lore Of Light: the stories of the prophets from Adam ¡ to Muhammad drawn from traditional Ottoman sources. This book is intended to be read aloud to young children and to be read by older children for themselves. The stories are shortened and simplified but not changed. The intention is to introduce young children to their prophets and to encourage thought and discussion in the family about the eternal wisdom these stories embody.

THE HONOR OF WOMEN IN ISLAM

Scholars in Islam Series

By Professor Yusuf da Costa

ISBN 1-930409-06-0 (2002) Paperback 104 pp.

Relying explicitly on Islamic source texts, this concise, scholarly work elucidates the true respect and love for women inherent in the Islamic faith. It examines the pre-Islamic state of women, highlights the unprecedented rights they received under Islamic Law, and addresses the prominent beliefs and prevailing cultures throughout the Muslim world regarding the roles of women in familial, social service and community development, business, academic, religious, and even judicial circles. In addition, brief case studies of historical figures such as Mary, mother of Jesus and Hagar, handmaiden of Sarah are presented within the Islamic tradition. An excellent resource for academics, policymakers, theologians, laypersons, and service providers.

IN THE MYSTIC FOOTSTEPS OF SAINTS

Sufi Wisdom Series

By Shaykh Muhammad Nazim Adil al-Haqqani

Volume 1–ISBN 1-930409-05-2 (2002) Paperback
Volume 2–ISBN 1-930409-09-5 (2002) Paperback
Volume 3–ISBN 1-930409-13-3 (2004) Paperback
Volume 4–ISBN 1-930409-13-3 (2004) Paperback

Narrated in a charming, old-world storytelling style, this highly spiritual series offers several volumes of practical guidance on how to establish serenity and peace in daily life, how to heal from emotional and spiritual scars, and discover the role we are each destined to play in the universal scheme. Written by Shaykh Nazim Adil al-Haqqani, worldwide leader of the Naqshbandi-Haqqani Sufi Order and a descendant of best-selling poet and Sufi mystic Jalaluddin Rumi. Average length 200 pp.

LIBERATING THE SOUL:

A Guide For Spiritual Growth

***Sufi Wisdom* Series**

By Shaykh Muhammad Nazim Adil al-Haqqani

Volume 1–ISBN 1-930409-14-1 (2002) Paperback
Volume 2–ISBN 1-930409-15-X (2002) Paperback
Volume 3–ISBN 1-930409-16-8 (2004) Paperback
Volume 4–ISBN 1-930409-17-6 (2004) Paperback

This series focuses on classical Sufi teachings, which open the heart to receive life-altering spiritual powers. *Liberating The Soul* is based on coveted lectures of Shaykh Muhammad Nazim Adil al-Haqqani, the worldwide leader of the Naqshbandi Sufi Order and descendant of best-selling poet Jalaluddin Rumi. Self-improvement and empowerment through spiritual discipline is a running theme. Topics include practical steps to rid the heart of doubt; build self-confidence in one's unique identity; overcome bad characteristics such as anger, greed, and jealousy; express gratitude for unlimited divine bounty; develop intimate communion with the Creator; learn to respect and appreciate all creation, develop tolerance for others; and much more. Average length 300 pp.

ENCYCLOPEDIA OF ISLAMIC DOCTRINE, VOL. 1-7

Shaykh Muhammad Hisham Kabbani

ISBN: 1-871031-86-9, Paperback.

The most comprehensive treatise on Islamic belief in the English language. Contemporary issues - absolutely essential for every Muslim household! The only work of its kind in the English language, Shaykh Hisham Kabbani's seven volume *Encyclopedia of Islamic Doctrine* is a monumental work covering in great detail the subtle points of Islamic belief and practice. Based on the four canonical schools of thought, this is an excellent and vital resource to anyone seriously interested in spirituality. There is no doubt that in retrospect, this will be the most significant work of this age.

Book 1: Beliefs (229 Pages)

Book 2: Remembrance of Allah and Praising the Prophet (225 Pages)

Book 3: The Prophet: Commemorations, Visitation and His Knowledge of the Unseen (191 Pages)

Book 4: Intercession (181 Pages)

Book 5: Self-Purification and the State of Excellence (192 Pages)

Book 6: Forgotten Aspects of Islamic Worship, Part 1 (177 Pages)
Book 7: Forgotten Aspects of Islamic Worship, Part 2

LaVergne, TN USA
03 January 2011
210885LV00007B/149/A

9 781930 409187